BEAT IT, BURN IT, AND DROWN IT

WESTMINSTER PRESS BOOKS

BY

SUZANNE HILTON

Beat It, Burn It, and Drown It
It's a Model World
It's Smart to Use a Dummy
How Do They Cope With It?
How Do They Get Rid of It?

BEAT IT, BURN IT, AND DROWN IT

by

SUZANNE HILTON

THE WESTMINSTER PRESS

Philadelphia

BOOK DESIGN BY
DOROTHY ALDEN SMITH

PUBLISHED BY THE WESTMINSTER PRESS®
PHILADELPHIA, PENNSYLVANIA

PRINTED IN THE UNITED STATES OF AMERICA

Library of Congress Cataloging in Publication Data

Hilton, Suzanne.
    Beat it, burn it, and drown it.

    Bibliography: p.
    SUMMARY: Examines the ways of testing materials
to ensure progress, safety, and quality of products.
    1. Testing—Juvenile Literature. [1. Testing.
2. Technology] I. Title.
TA410.H48   620′.004′4   73–11318
ISBN 0–664–32538–6

CONTENTS

(*Continued on next page*)

Research is something that
if you don't do it 'till you have to,
it's too late

—CHARLES F. KETTERING

INTRODUCTION

"LABORATORY TESTS prove that . . ."

Several times a day, radio and television commercials claim that their tests prove the products they advertise are better than the Brand X's of the world. Perhaps one product *is* better than another—but the "tests" you see on television are not the ones that prove anything!

This is a book about what laboratory tests really prove. And what they cannot prove.

The tests are of all kinds. Some products are beaten up, burned, deluged with water, and even broken. Some may be twisted, shaken, squeezed, stretched, and bent a little. Others are taken apart bit by bit, and some may not get hurt at all. While many products receive just a few of those abuses, others get every one—plus a few more original ideas that people think of adding.

But it is all for a very important reason. Testing helps to make everything we buy safer and more useful.

What makes the difference between the tests mentioned in this book and some of the tests shown on commercials is that real testers use scientific methods. Holding a match near a piece of clothing or rug to see whether it will burn is not a real test. But exposing the material to a flame at a *certain* distance, for a *certain* length of time, under *certain* conditions of temperature and humidity makes it a scientific test.

Scientific tests are tough because products have to pass them before they can measure up to the standards already set by the Government or Government-approved groups. Setting standards keeps progress from going backward. Each time a product or an invention is changed a little, that product or invention must be better than the one it replaces.

Before the seventeenth century, testing was hit-or-miss rather than scientific. Few records were kept, so many inventions disappeared almost as soon as they appeared. Then they would reappear a few centuries later, only to vanish again. All through history the diving bell kept popping up that way. About 334 B.C., Philip of Macedon's men built a "glass" barrel and lowered it to the bottom of the sea. Almost every country along a warm seacoast tried diving bells of one sort or another. In 1972, the U.S. Navy perfected one with an acrylic hull that is much like the one the Macedonians had in mind. Only this time, the invention will not disappear again.

Scientific testing and record-keeping began about 335 years ago when a brilliant man named Galileo showed people how to test everything first —then throw away the bad ideas and keep the good ones. Today scientists still use Galileo's good ideas, but they have improved greatly on his methods. Testing is more important than it ever was.

The youngster who spends his last quarter on a pen that won't write or on a candy bar that has a worm in it is every bit as disappointed as the parent who spends $3,000 on a car that's a lemon. Perhaps they would have been happier if they had known what laboratory tests *really* prove.

1

Shock and impact testing

BEAT IT

GALILEO'S housekeeper sighed when he heard the news. Galileo Galilei had so many projects going on that his study was always a mess. Now, to make matters worse, he would never leave his house again.

Galileo had been on the losing side of an argument with the church leaders of his day. Instead of agreeing with them that the sun revolved around the earth, he had said it was the other way around: the earth moves around the sun. But the churchmen were too powerful for him. They settled the problem once and for all by sentencing Galileo to spend the rest of his life in his own house.

A month later, his housekeeper thought, Galileo was just as stubborn and peppery as ever. When the roof of a friend's housed caved in, Galileo refused to believe it was an "act of God." There had to be another reason, he insisted. The roof beam had not been strong enough or the house had not been built properly.

Everything built by man is subject to certain forces, Galileo said. Some-times those forces are strong enough to make the material break. If only a builder had some way of knowing how strong his materials were before he built a house or a bridge, he would not make mistakes by choosing the weaker materials. Galileo was lost in thought for a while.

A few days later his friends began hauling in heavy wooden beams, chains, weights, metals, and all kinds of materials to build with. In a few hours the place looked like a junkyard. Galileo was happier than he had been in months. Only his body was confined to the house. His brain was still free. He began building machines the like of which no one had ever seen before.

"What are they for?" his friends protested. "Are they for making something?"

Galileo showed them how the machines helped him test different materials. He dropped a weight down on an oak plank. It didn't break. Then he dropped the same weight on a pine plank and it broke in half.

"That's no surprise," his audience

9

argued. "We always knew that oak was stronger than pine."

"But we never knew how *much* stronger," Galileo told them, pointing to the gauges that had measured the force of the weight.

Next he had his housekeeper help to hoist another plank to the ceiling so that it hung suspended in air. Galileo began attaching weights to the free end. First a 100-pound weight; then 300 pounds more.

"As long as the stress is running the length of the board, it can take a great deal of weight."

Galileo had attached 1,000 pounds of weights and still the board showed no signs of cracking. Finally he had his housekeeper lower the plank. He laid it across two barrels, one barrel supporting each end.

"Now the stress would be different if I put weights in the middle of the board," he explained to his friends. "A small child could break it."

Galileo put a 40-pound weight in the center of the board. It sagged. When he added another 10 pounds, the board broke.

The whole idea was too new to be understood all at once. Galileo's friends left the house worried that his life sentence had perhaps affected his brain after all. But Galileo was busy measuring the strengths of other materials besides wood. For months the banging and clanging in Galileo's house was deafening, but finally there came quiet moments too. These came when he was writing his discoveries in

10

a book called *Dialogues Concerning Two New Sciences.*

The book was to change the world of science. In those days engineers had been called "mechanical philosophers." From now on they would be scientists. And because of his experiments, Galileo has had a little part in everything made and tested since 1638—from cereal boxes to lunar modules.

Today almost everything that man makes has to be tested. More products are getting beaten up, bumped, scraped, and dropped in one day than Galileo ever owned in his life.

One of the ways to test a product is to see how much shock and impact it can take. Every time a body strikes against another one, there is an impact. It may be such a small impact that there is not even a scrape. It may be a fall, as when an article is dropped or thrown. Or it may be a very hard blow. There are all kinds of impacts. But when there is a violent collision—as when one body hits against another very hard—the impact is so strong that there is shock also.

A package of gelatin dessert mix has to be tough to make it all the way from its manufacturer to the grocery store shelf. If it's not, the contents will spill out and no one will ever buy it. So before the trip starts, the manufacturer treats his boxes of gelatin (and all his other products) to a "pretend" train or truck trip. Those which travel by train will have to survive many bumps like the slams that train cars make when they crash together during starts and stops. Gelatin boxes, jars of peanut butter, bags of potato chips—all take a ride down a ramp, bouncing against a wooden wall to prove they are well designed. Of course, not every single package has to be tested. Whenever a new type of package is designed, samples of it must take the test. Or when a grocery manager complains, "all your packages arrived broken," the manufacturer tests his packages again.

Tests for packages—and for every other product in this book—include many different kinds of tests. The same packages have to be tested in various ways to see how well they can stand being wiggled and jiggled, squeezed and smashed, burned and drowned. But those tests are in later chapters.

Most cameras are tested for impact very gently because they are delicate instruments. But there is one camera that gets dropped, thrown around, forced to operate for three weeks without a rest, and even shot at. It's the surveillance camera that works in a bank. There it is expected to take perfect pictures even though the lighting is the worst that any camera has to put up with. It must work in complete silence, since its main job is to photograph bank robbers, who do not like their pictures taken—especially when they are robbing the bank.

Once, when a camera was spotted by an angry robber, he ripped it off the wall and threw it into a flower box. From there, the camera continued to grind away, taking the gunman's picture nicely framed by ferns. Another

A carton of gelatin about to receive an impact

GENERAL FOODS CORP.

camera was hit by the bullet of a camera-shy gunman. But tests had prepared the camera for this sort of thing, and it kept right on taking pictures. The cameras are so good they usually get 50 to 100 photos of the robbery going on. Over 90 percent of the robberies in banks that have surveillance cameras are solved.

The violent impact that hits a parachute when the air suddenly opens it is a kind of shock. After World War II, some of the same men who had been parachuting from burning planes or onto battlefields thought how nice it might be to try jumping in a peaceful sky for a change. Sport parachuting became popular before there were any sports parachutes. Some of the more daring jumpers carried along scissors and snipped slots in their nylon canopies to make them more maneuverable. This designing of chutes by do-it-yourselfers was no way to a happy landing. One company decided that it was time

11

A new gliding parachute takes a violent impact when it first opens

PIONEER PARACHUTE CO., INC.

more tests. Then come the shocks. A chute opening with 400 pounds of weight when it is traveling at 200 mph has a shock force of 5,000 pounds. The manufacturer, using either an airplane or a whirl tower, makes this shock as high as 9,000 pounds just to make certain his parachute will pass the required tests.

Telephone linemen have different up-in-the-air problems. When this century began, impact on their own heads was one of their biggest worries. The telephone had been invented a long time before, but only rich people could afford one. Now phones had become much cheaper and everyone wanted one in his home. Linemen were on every street setting up poles and stringing

to start making a new kind of chute.

Each skydiver must wear two chutes —a main chute on his back and an auxiliary (or emergency) one on his chest. He is allowed to pack one of them himself, but the other must be packed by a Federal inspector. All sports parachutes have to pass some rugged tests—mostly to see if they can stand up to the shock of opening up. First there are 12 tests with a 170-pound dummy. When dropped (by airplane) from 500 feet, the chutes must open fully in three seconds. The chutes are packed with twists in them for five

12

This "bomb" holds a new type of parachute to be tested

PIONEER PARACHUTE CO., INC.

wires. But the work was unfamiliar, and no one has ever discovered a way to keep men from dropping their tools. This was very hard on the heads of the men who worked below.

Workmen stuffed their derby hats with crumpled newspaper and everything else they could think of to protect their skulls. But nothing they used for stuffing was tough enough. World War I gave some of the men an idea. Why not use a metal helmet like the ones soldiers wore? The few linemen who could locate steel helmets found out why not. Wearing a metal hat where there were wires was even worse than just getting hit on the head. Now they could be electrocuted too. Besides, when a metal tool dropped on a metal helmet, the clang nearly deafened the wearer. The helmets were too heavy and fell off easily. The world was ready for someone to invent a good hard hat.

When a brand-new invention comes along it does not run into competition, because there is no other product like it. Also, no standards have yet been set for it to meet. The new invention sets the first standards itself. The first standard for a hard hat was that it must be hard enough to be hit by a dropped hammer and still protect its wearer from any head injury. The next standard was that it could not be metal, or at least must not conduct electricity. A third standard says that it must be of lightweight material. Soon firemen wanted to use the new hat, so another standard was added—it must be fireproof. Other standards were set after

tests showed that more safeguards were needed.

One of the tests for a hard hat is to drop a 1-pound weight (about what a hatchet weighs) onto the hat from a height of 10 feet. If it doesn't make a dent deeper than a quarter of an inch, the hat is safe to wear. But first another standard had to be set. If a hatchet makes a quarter-inch dent in a hat, it will not be safe to wear that hat snugly against the head. So another standard was set for the hard hat. The workman must be fitted with a headband that keeps his hard hat away from his head on all sides. Standards are set to pro-

New laws will see that motorcycle helmets are tested more carefully—even though the rider is only on a minicycle

tect people from poor products, and standard tests are set to make sure that a workman in Idaho or Texas wears a helmet that has been tested as carefully as the one worn by a workman in Hawaii or Maine.

Motorcycle riders are not so lucky. They still cannot be certain their helmets are safe. One state study of motorcycle accidents showed that three fourths of the cyclists killed had died of head injuries. And many of them had been wearing helmets. But no one had ever set standards for motorcycle helmets. Each manufacturer made what he thought was a good one. Some really were good. But others were not at all safe, even though their labels stated that they had been "tested." A test does not mean much if it is not a standard test or one that is approved by a nationally known testing company.

How many rubs make a hole in a piece of upholstery material? A textile technician finds out

GOOD HOUSEKEEPING INSTITUTE

14

Not all impact tests have to be hammer-dropping tough. When a manufacturer of blue jeans discovered that his dungarees did not last as well as those made by a competitor, he sent samples of the material to a laboratory for abrasion tests. Abrasion is another kind of impact—the kind that happens when a youngster's knee wears a hole through his jeans.

A 6-inch-square piece of material was attached to a machine. A piece of emery cloth (like sandpaper) rubbed hard against the sample of denim material and soon a hole appeared. The lab tester tried a much heavier piece of denim. This time it took many more rubs, but the hole finally showed up in that piece too. For the last test, the tester took a piece of jeans material made with nylon thread. This time there were 6,000 rubs before a hole appeared. Now the manufacturer could decide whether to go on making dungarees that wore out quickly or add nylon thread to the fabric of his jeans to make them last longer.

When it is time to test a product, some manufacturers test their own. But testing laboratories are expensive, and not every company can have one. There are many commercial laboratories that do every kind of testing. Any manufacturer can send his products to a testing laboratory to find out all about them. Some labs test anything and everything. Others test only certain kinds of products. Still others specialize in certain types of testing—like environmental testing or electrical testing. After the tests have been made, the lab sends the manufacturer a "report card" to tell him how well his product has done. The testing lab really tells the truth about a product, and the truth is what the manufacturer wants to know.

The impact tests done on a bicycle may vary widely, depending on who does them. The manufacturer wants to be sure his bicycle is ready for what lies ahead by testing every mechanical part carefully. He chooses a few from the assembly line and tells his testers to give them a rough time. They will test the frame, the gears, the brakes, the lights, the wheels.

When the bicycle's report card comes back, it may have some very bad marks as well as some very good ones. Suppose the testers found that the bike's brakes would fail after 100 hours' use? If the maker is a good one, he will design better brakes for the

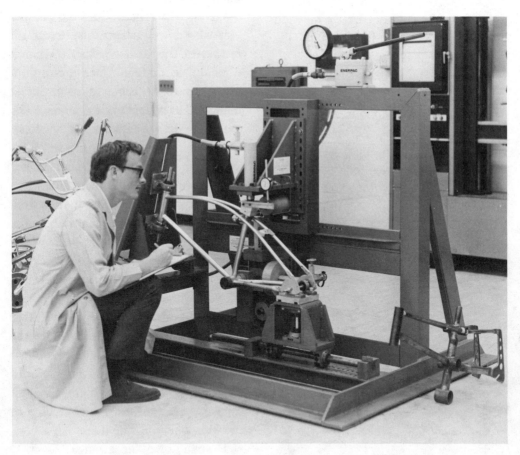

A bicycle manufacturer invents a machine to test the bicycle frame

AMF INC.

Some riders test bicycles in ways their makers never thought of

CONSUMERS UNION

bike. But if he doesn't care, he may sell the bicycle the way it is and let the buyer worry.

"Let the buyer beware" was an everyday saying until a few years ago. It meant, "After you buy a product, it's your problem if it falls apart."

Buyers soon grew angry about having to beware. They felt that when they had paid good money for some-

Not all bicycle seats are alike

CONSUMERS UNION

16

thing, such as a bicycle, they had a right to expect it to last for a while—if they took good care of it. Most manufacturers are honest, but there are a few who are not. Angry buyers decided to form groups to protect people from careless manufacturers. These groups are called consumer groups.

The Consumers Union is just one of those consumer groups. It makes its own tests to help people decide what products to buy. These tests are often quite different from those made by the manufacturer. The Consumers Union never accepts money from the companies whose products it tests, because it must feel free to say exactly what it thinks of a product. Since it is a nonprofit group, it began a magazine it could sell to people to raise money. The magazine tells people about the tests made each month on different products. The report does not actually say one product is better than another—only that some passed certain tests well, some not so well, and some came close to flunking. The decision of which product to buy is left up to each person.

The trials waiting for a bicycle when the Consumers Union tests it are very different from those the bicycle maker used. One difference is the company the bike keeps. For the first time, it is tested with many other bikes from factories all over the world. Also for the first time, the bike comes into contact with the kids who will ride it.

Humans often do strange things to bicycles—things the manufacturer did not expect the riders to do. They bounce up over 5-inch curbs. They ride their friends on the handlebars or on the seats that were designed to hold just one rider. Instead of using kickstands, they drop their bikes on the ground at every stop. They jounce mercilessly up and down on seats that may have just the bare minimum of padding for absorbing shock. The Consumers Union tests are meant to give the bicycles the hardest sort of workout they will meet out in the street:

The wheels will thump 6,000 times in 1 hour over a steel "bump" attached to the treadmill the bike rides on. Weights are attached to the seat, then to the handlebars, to see how the bike will adjust to different loads. The brakes are tested. Some work perfectly, others collapse after 100 uses, while still others are no good at all until they have been used 50 times. Some bikes do not have ball bearing steering, and in the Consumers Union magazine bicycle buyers are warned not to try riding these "no hands." After the tests are completed, some of the bicycles can hardly make it to the scrap heap. All this testing proves much that the manufacturers are glad to learn—and bike buyers too.

Where the snow is deep, bicycles are sometimes replaced by a newcomer, the snowmobile. Actually snowmobiles arrived very suddenly one winter recently —before they had been tested quite enough. Snow is very deceiving. It looks too soft to create a very hard impact, but that first winter snowmobile riders had an unusual number of backaches. When a snowmobile zooms over the brow of a hill it takes to the air for a thrilling moment. Then comes the impact—when the riders plop back hard on their seats.

Snowmobile makers realized they had better get to the bottom of the matter before they would be sued by the riders for back injuries. The manufacturers built an impacter in the shape of the passenger's rear. Then they calculated the force that a rider might hit when he dropped back down on the seat after zinging out over a hill. The force was six times as great as had been expected. When the impacter hit the snowmobile seat with that same force, it went clear through the seat. Then the testers tried it on a seat of all foam, but the same thing happened. That impacter slammed down many times be-

A snowmobile seat is sometimes a crash pad

GOODYEAR TIRE & RUBBER CO.

17

fore the testers found a combination of several kinds of foam that would break the snowmobile rider's hard landing.

If sports equipment were not carefully tested, a sport would be just a game where skill means very little. A bowling ball has to take quite a beating, and impact tests give the manufacturer a chance to try out new materials. Finding the right material that will be tough enough to last, weigh just the allowable weight, and still be perfectly balanced takes many tests. The testers have to build a machine to simulate the bowler's roll so that each roll will be exactly the same. A ski boot is another piece of athletic equipment that takes a specially hard beating. Since their boots are often blamed by the skiers if they break a leg on the slopes, ski boot manufacturers keep trying to make better-fitting boots that can hold up under the roughest conditions.

Indoor track stars were happy when they heard rumors that the hardwood floors in arenas might be changed. The impact of their feet on the track made their feet so hot that they usually suffered from blisters. The runners felt that almost any change would be welcome.

Engineers invented a Rube Goldberg device to test ski boots
AMF INC.

First there had to be tests to be sure the new surface would be acceptable for racing competition. Artificial turf had already been used around swimming pools, for football fields, as a divider strip on highways, and for children's playgrounds. But no one had ever tried using it for a track. Testers attached thermocouples to some joggers' shoes and sent the men around an artificial turf track first. The thermocouples, which measure heat, showed that there was far less heat than on a wooden track. Then the joggers said their legs were not even tired. At last runners had their chance to try it. No blisters! What's more, they found they did not even slip as they had on the wooden floor.

One large arena was built recently with the track made of artificial turf. One of the first races during the opening week proved that the tests had been successful. A star runner beat the world's indoor 3-mile speed record.

Impact tests were an important part of a new invention for the kitchen. A few years ago, the family dishwasher (the kind with two legs and an apron) hated to wash the frying pan because everything stuck to it. Then an engineer invented Teflon lining. The new frying pan was the easiest one to wash, but, as with many new inventions, there was a catch to it. Metal tools used in the frying pan scratched the lining badly.

The best solution, the laboratory testers said, was to tell buyers to use only wooden or plastic tools with Teflon-lined pans. Some cooks complained that using those tools was like "trying to turn over a fried egg with a cooked noodle." Meanwhile the impact tests continued. Researchers tested new tools, new coatings, and new ways to put on the Teflon. At last they were rewarded. There had been nothing wrong with the Teflon coating—only that it was put on wrong. The impact tests continued even after that discovery, but this time the impacts made no scratches. The new coating was called Teflon II.

While mother cooks with her new pans, her children may be doing a little impact-testing of their own. Toys can sometimes turn into dangerous enemies in the hands of children. Some toys have sharp points that cut or stab. Some have small pieces that could choke a child. Parents and baby-sitters cannot always be on the spot when a toy breaks. They cannot go into a toy store and drop and throw toys to find out which could be dangerous. What can they do?

A new law forbids the sale of dangerous toys. But first there had to be a way to find out which toys were dangerous. The Food and Drug Administration's Bureau of Product Safety helped here. The members set up a system with 130 hospitals throughout the country to report every single accident involving a child and a toy. (After the first year, bicycles, as a cause, were way ahead—especially when used in the street.) They also appointed a toy review committee that included two engineers, a doctor, and an injury data

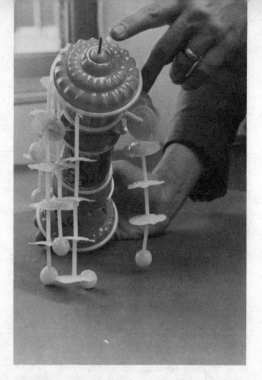

A baby's toy fails the test when a sharp point is uncovered

expert. They gave the toys they checked over quite a beating.

Anyone can use the impact tests the Bureau used to find dangerous toys. But try them at home—not in a toy store! A toy to be used by a child up to eighteen months old should be "drop-tested" 10 times from a height of 4½ feet (about the height of a high-chair). Each time the toy is dropped, it should be in a slightly different position. A toy for an older child is dropped only 4 times from a height of 3 feet. The reason for this difference is that an older child is not so likely to drop his toy as he is to bite, twist, or bend it.

Meanwhile, many other groups helped to fight this war on dangerous toys. The Toy Manufacturers of America began to set standards—for the

first time—for toy manufacturers to follow. The Consumers Union tested toys and even took some to court to show judges that they were too hazardous for the playroom. More new laws say that the manufacturer must put a warning label on some toys, so parents can see that they might be dangerous to their children.

One of the groups that test toys and other products bought for use at home began as a magazine for homemakers. By 1885, the industrial revolution had started making American homelife entirely different. People no longer had to braid rags to make rugs for their houses. They could stop weaving their own materials to make clothes. Machines were invented to do the hard work. Almost everything could be bought in stores.

That year, Clark W. Bryan started a magazine to help people know what products to buy for their homes. But the job was not so easy as Mr. Bryan had thought. There were too many products. And there was no way to tell which were the best unless he tested them all. So, a few years later, his magazine started a laboratory. In that laboratory, he planned to test every single item that would be advertised in his magazine, *Good Housekeeping*.

The Good Housekeeping Institute can be very rough in testing products. For instance, rugs. There are so many new kinds of carpet today that their testers had to take samples of 5,000 different rugs to see which were the toughest. One machine presses down

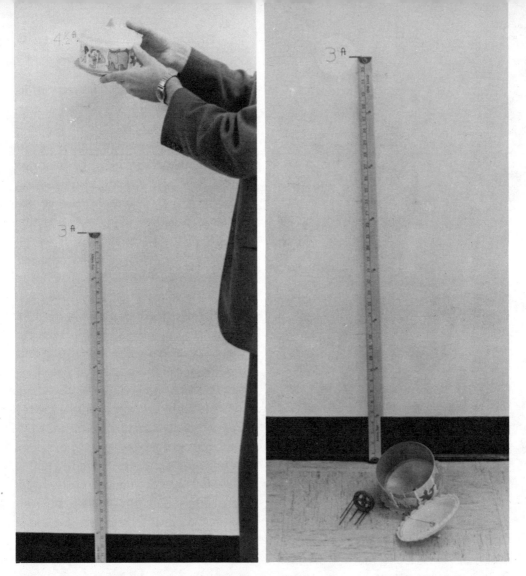

A musical toy gets the drop test . . .
. . . and suddenly becomes three pieces—all dangerous

U.S. BUREAU OF PRODUCT SAFETY

the pile of the carpet to see how footsteps or furniture legs will rub down the rug in a house. Another machine yanks at the tufts to make sure they are firm. Still another pounds a rug sample for 4 hours to see how much abrasion it can take. A vacuum cleaner runs back and forth across each sample 4,000 times to see whether the rug sheds. All sorts of stains are dropped on the samples, and several kinds of cleaning fluids are swabbed on to clean them up. Finally, large squares of each kind of rug—the finalists in the contest —are set down in a carpet aisle. Twenty thousand people will walk over them before they are taken up to see how well they resisted dirt and wear.

Which mattress to buy is another difficult choice for a homemaker to make.

21

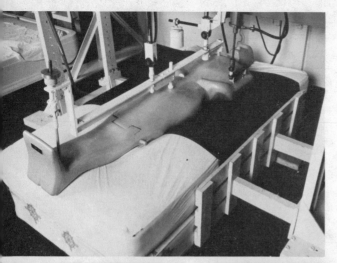

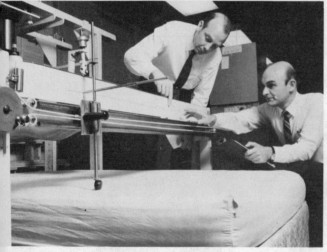

Sebastian, the dummy, applies dynamic fatigue to a mattress as he tosses, turns, and twists . . .

Afterward, engineers check the mattress for damage

After sleeping one night on it, anyone can tell whether it is good or not. But stores do not allow people to try out their mattresses first. The Good Housekeeping Institute keeps a mechanical man, Sebastian, who is a very poor sleeper. For hours, Sebastian twists and turns the way most people do in

their sleep. In a day, he can show testers what would happen to a mattress during a whole year of use in a home. Just like every product advertised in the magazine, the mattress must pass the Good Housekeeping Institute's tests before it can be advertised. Another requirement is that the product must be able to do everything that its label claims it can do. Some companies send their products to the Institute in the hope that they can win the Good Housekeeping Seal of Approval. To earn the right to use the seal for a year on the advertising, the products take more tests, because if they fail after they are bought by a customer, the Institute guarantees to pay the consumer for the money he lost.

Fifty years ago anyone who took a day's journey by car could expect to have at least one flat tire on the way. That was before the tire-torture tests that are designed for today's cars.

A cobblestone course tests the new steel-belted tire against other kinds of tires

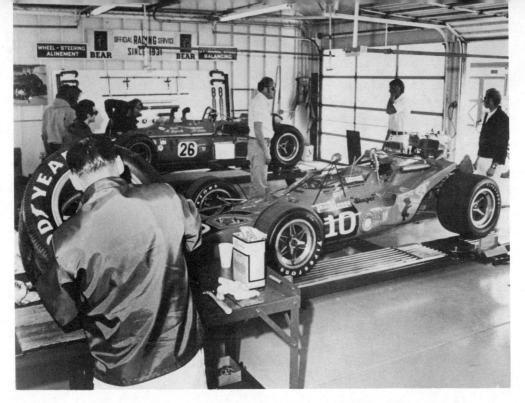

Racing cars are tested carefully before the Indianapolis 500

The impact of the tire on the road is what wears tires out. But some tire companies are not satisfied to test their tires on ordinary roads only. The companies build a special road of cobblestones or sharp rocks to give their tires the hardest trip they may ever have. That was one way they tested the new steel-belted tires to see how much better they are than other kinds of tires. Another impact on the road occurs when the driver hits potholes. In order to learn how well a tire can stand up for a driver who manages to hit every hole in the road, the testing engineers attach a steel bump to the spinning flywheel (which acts as the road for this test). The tire rides along this "road" until gradually the bump wears down a portion of the tire. Some types of

tires last many miles more than others.

A racing-car driver is not looking for the tire that goes the most miles when he tests tires. A perfectly balanced racing car can mean the difference between winning and losing. He tests tires until he finds four that are so perfectly balanced under the car that they will make a whole mile per hour difference and can win the race for him.

When an airplane's wheels first hit the runway, there are two huge impacts. One is the impact the wheels take in landing on the hard concrete. Aircraft companies test their landing wheels hundreds of times before they are satisfied that a wheel is strong enough to stand that kind of slamming around.

23

The main landing wheels for a new jumbo jet are installed in a drop tower to test how they behave during landings

Two kinds of lunar landers have very different tests. Children handle the testing of this one

24

The other impact is one that no one thought much about until recently. That is the impact that the wheel gives to the airport runway. Runways had always been built of concrete—very much as some roads are made. Now airports all over the world are finding that their concrete runways are crumbling. Airport managers decided it was time to find out why and what could be done about it.

To solve the case of the battered runways plenty of testing was involved. Testers had just about agreed that the problem must be caused by those big jumbo jets when they discovered they were wrong. Many types of smaller airplanes are harder on the concrete runway than are the big planes. The difference is not in the size of the plane but in the way the wheels are loaded. The load on just one wheel of a plane runs from almost 42,000 pounds (for a B-747) to over 52,000 pounds (for a DC-10). That heavy a load dropping down on a small area of concrete was bound to cause trouble.

What airports really needed was something better than ordinary highway concrete for planes to land on. A flexible concrete would be better. Testers began trying out various kinds of

Space engineers get ready for a drop test of the real lunar module. From a safety blockhouse (in foreground) *they can monitor the "landing" on TV*

GRUMMAN AEROSPACE CORP.

concrete—some that had not even been placed on the market yet. They used heavy weights to simulate the wheels of landing planes as well as vibrations to simulate the shaking that a jumbo jet gives the runway when it lands.

Finally they tried mixing concrete with steel fibers—one kind of material that had not been tried yet. The new fibrous concrete was exactly what they needed. But they had to make tests to see how much better the new kind of material was. They built a machine to simulate an airplane landing wheel weighing 30,000 pounds. The new concrete lasted four times as long as the old concrete, but it cracked after 4,000 landings. Could it be repaired? They made it twice as thick and it stood up twice as long. At last they were satisfied. The new concrete is now being laid in airports around the world.

Meanwhile, space engineers were working on a problem that was keeping them awake nights. It concerned the most important impact in centuries —the moment the lunar module would impact on the moon. Just suppose, they moaned, everything should go perfectly until the last 42 inches! Who knew exactly what the moon's surface held in store? What if, at the last second, the lunar module's leg would collapse or slip off a rock and the LEM fall over on its side?

Engineers had tested every single item that went into the LEM. And every piece of material used to build it. But still the testers figured there were nine things that could possibly go

25

wrong in those last seconds before the lunar module's feet rested firmly on lunar soil. They had to test those nine possibilities.

First they built a huge frame to hold the simulated lunar lander in place. It was a full-sized scale model weighing 15,000 pounds and balanced exactly as the real module would be. It could be hoisted up and dropped—at first only 1½ inches, then more, until one drop was from 42 inches. Each time the places where the legs were to touch down were changed to slope at different angles. That was in case the module landed on a crater slope or on a rock. Eighteen times it was dropped down to land different ways. One time a man was aboard to make sure the crew's seat belts would hold them safely.

The most critical moment on each of the drop tests was during a few milliseconds at impact. A millisecond is less time than it would have taken Galileo to say "Go."

2

Testing with fire

BURN IT

Since the first caveman carried a burning stick into his cave, man has thought he could control fire. But he can't always.

Actually man has really never learned enough about fire. That is why so many tests are being made to learn more about fires, how they can be discovered in time, how they can be put out, and especially how they can be stopped before they start.

One way people learn more about fires is to test them in special laboratories. A forest fire lab tests ways to control and prevent fires in a natural environment. An insurance company's lab tests the kinds of fires its customers may have. A Navy lab tests shipboard fires and ways to fight them when there is a shortage of fresh water aboard. An explosion lab tests explosive fires that can begin with something that seems quite harmless, like lint or powdered sugar.

A special kind of laboratory at the U.S. Bureau of Mines tests coal mine explosions. In the old days, miners felt safe if they carred a canary with them

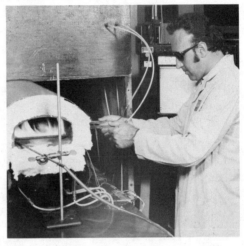

This special oven can show a scientist just what would happen to any kind of material in any type of fire

AVCO CORP.

into the mines to warn them of gas. If there was any gas in the mine, the bird would keel over quickly, and the miners knew it was time to get out of the mine fast. But they never suspected, until after some unexplained explosions, that gas was not their only enemy in the mine. Sometimes a gas explosion occurred in a remote corner of the mine, yet explosive fires ripped into

27

Fortunately this explosion is only a test—to help develop new safety materials for coal mines

U.S. BUREAU OF MINES

every corridor. Why? Coal dust! The black powdery stuff that comes off coal as it is broken into chunks is highly explosive. One spark is enough to ignite every tiny grain of the dust. Coal dust explosions—and ways to control them—are tested in the Bureau of Mines experimental coal mine. It has been the scene of 3,000 explosions already!

Another laboratory began back in the days when electricity was still brand new to most people. Twenty-two years before, most of the city of Chicago had burned down. People in other parts of the country thought Chicago was finished, but they didn't know Chicago people. Not only was the city rebuilt, but it was the host of a tremendous fair —the World's Columbian Exposition of 1893. That fair was the scene of a lot of "firsts." There was a giant Ferris wheel, for one. Another "first" that impressed men more than women was the

28

electrified third rail. People talked about something new called a "subway" that might put the horse-drawn trolley car out of business. But the biggest eye-popper of them all was the Palace of Electricity. When it was lighted up at night, it could be seen for miles.

The Palace of Electricity had its problems, though, for those people who worked backstage. The truth was that electrical wiring was so new that no one knew how to do it right. As a result, the Palace had so many small electrical fires that the insurance underwriters of the Exposition had to hire one young man full time just to find out what was causing the fires and to study ways to put out electrical fires. William Henry Merrill followed many fire engines that summer studying fires. At last he learned how to untangle the wire mess at the Palace and how to put out a fire once it began.

After the Exposition was over, the fire insurance underwriters asked Merrill to stay longer. By now, he and his team of researchers were the only experts around on the subject of electrical fires. Besides, the fair had made people so excited about electricity that companies sprang up almost overnight making new electrical products. Some were well made and safe, but others were made so badly that they were very dangerous. Merrill's laboratory became known as the Underwriters' Laboratories.

From the very beginning, local manufacturers sent their products to Merrill and asked him to test them. At first they were only electrical products, but before long he was testing all sorts of products for fire and other hazards. Very soon the lab in the spare room over the firehouse was too small. Merrill needed a huge furnace, for one thing, where he could test "fire doors" and other large items that were supposed to be fireproof.

Today, a person walking into the five laboratories of the company might see all sorts of testing. A new kind of floor-to-ceiling construction, as large as a room, is being lowered over a furnace where it will be tested to see how fire-resistant it is. A man is attacking a burglar-resistant safe with torches, sledgehammers, chisels, and drills to find out whether it really is resistant. Another man is overloading some electrical wires to see whether he can start a fire.

When the laboratories approve of a product, after thorough testing and investigation, then that product may wear the UL seal of approval.

But people cannot do all their fire-studying in a lab. Sometimes learning about fire has to be done right on the scene of a fire—a fire that has been set on purpose.

One of the most dangerous of modern fires is the fire that occurs in a high-rise building. A tall building can hold as many people as a medium-sized city. How can they all get out? The fire codes in a city say that a tall building must have a stairway so the people can escape in case of fire. The code looks fine on paper, but in actual practice it does not always work.

Suddenly an office wastebasket catches fire, and before anyone notices, fire has spread to draperies and paper on the desks. People begin running toward the stairway. But when they open the stairway door, the smoke follows them. They soon find that their avenue of escape has turned into a chimney. The stairway is filled with the very smoke and gases they are trying to escape. People from the floors above cannot get past the floor where the fire is because of the smoke rushing up toward them. The elevators are useless because they work electronically. Many elevator call buttons are activated by the heat of a person's finger. But the heat of a fire also makes the call button work. All the elevators in the building move to the floor where the fire is, open their doors, and stay there. Any person who happens to be in the elevator at the time gets a firsthand look at a scorching blaze.

Is there a way to make the stairways safe during a fire? Many researchers thought they knew ways. One of the best suggestions was to pump fresh air into the stairwells with large fans. This would build up the air pressure. Then, when the doors were opened, fresh air would push into the room where the fire started. But it was only an idea. It could not be tested during a real fire, where many people's lives were at stake. So how could the researchers ever find out whether the plan would work?

29

The chance to learn more about fires in skyscrapers came when a 22-story New York City office building was to be torn down. It was the perfect laboratory to learn about fires in high-rise structures. Scientists from the Polytechnic Institute of Brooklyn and the firemen of New York City arranged the scene.

The old wooden desks on the two floors to be used for the tests were littered with papers—probably more so than most desks really are. Fans were put in the stairways to force air up from the bottom. This filled the stairways with fresh air. The fire chief lighted the match to start the flames. Sensors immediately began recording the temperature and air pressure in the room. Firemen and scientists used walkie-talkies to check with each other on the smoke and heat that reached the stairways. Meanwhile, air from the stairs helped to push the smoke and poisonous gases out of the raised windows. There was time for people to escape, and a safe stairway for them to use.

While one group of testers is trying to find out more about fires and what causes them, other researchers concentrate on testing the fire detectors and alarms that are supposed to warn people when there is a fire.

A fire chief in Minnesota was always being asked about fire detectors. Did they really detect fires? What kind was best? One day the chief decided to make some tests before he answered any more questions. He set six fires in one day and learned things about fire de-

The right kind of fire detector could have warned the owners of this burned-out shell in time to call firemen

DAVID LEARY/ABINGTON FIRE DEPT.

tectors—those small sensors that notice a fire before humans do—that even their manufacturers did not know.

When a small house in town was about to be torn down to make way for a supermarket the fire chief asked permission to make some tests. Besides, he added, firemen never get to see the start of a fire. They might learn quite a bit about how fires get going. And he had another reason for his last test, but he did not tell anyone about that yet.

The house was like many others in the neighborhood, with the living quarters on the first floor, a basement, and an extra bedroom in the attic. Fifteen fire detectors were put in the rooms. Some were the kind that "detect" as soon as there is a sudden change in the temperature—more than 15° F. They are called rate-of-rise detectors. Some "detect" the products of combustion—like the gases that are released even before smoke or flame appears. These

A 22-story building about to be torn down becomes the scene of an important fire

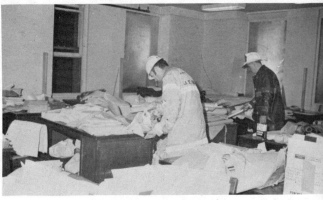

Firemen begin lighting the fire

Windows are open to help gases escape

The fire is out

In a smoky room nearby, instruments measure air pressure, heat, amount of smoke, and the gases from the fire

POLYTECHNIC INSTITUTE OF BROOKLYN
CENTER FOR URBAN ENVIRONMENTAL STUDIES

31

The burned-out hole in the living room floor is where a lady fell asleep on a couch—a lighted cigarette in her hand

TIMES-CHRONICLE, JENKINTOWN, PA.

are called ionization detectors. Another was a smoke detector. It detects a fire when smoke interferes with a light beam. The last detector was called a fixed-temperature detector. It is set to ring an alarm when the room reaches a certain temperature.

The stage was ready. Now the chief began setting his fires. He had chosen six of the fires that happen most often in homes. The results surprised even him.

The first fire was a smoldering one in the basement—the kind that starts all by itself in a pile of old paint rags or wet burlap bags tossed in a corner. Or the kind that starts in a sofa or bed when someone falls asleep while smoking. Firemen had often wondered how fast a smoldering fire became dangerous. Now they found out. In less than a minute the ionization detector (the one that detects fumes) set off the first alarm. There still had been no real

change in the temperature of the cellar, but now it began filling with smoke rapidly. Even when the basement was filled with smoke, people upstairs would never have known that a fire had started unless they had detectors. The firemen put out the fire (as they did in all the following tests) as soon as all the detectors had sounded their alarms.

An overheating old motor in a refrigerator started the second fire. This time it was twelve minutes before any alarm rang. Firemen noticed that having the bedroom door closed would have kept sleeping people safe for several minutes longer. During the next fire, the men left the bedroom door open just to see how fast the smoke traveled through the house. This third fire was caused by a frayed electric cord that ran under a rug and a stuffed chair in the living room. In ten minutes the smoke from this fire would have killed anyone in the bedroom.

A pan of hot bacon grease started the kitchen fire. The flames roared up from the stove and licked around some wooden cabinets and the wall. The ionization detector set off its alarm the same second that the fire was started. In four minutes the kitchen ceiling had reached a temperature too hot for humans to stand.

What happens when children play with matches and one drops into a kitchen wastebasket? It was hard for even the firemen to believe that one match could cause such a fire, until the chief made this test. At noon the match was dropped, and in less than one minute the first alarm sounded. In that minute, the temperature in the room reached 1,000° F.! Within a few seconds it had reached the heat that kills a human (over 300° F.). When the temperature reaches 630° F., grease in a room will ignite all by itself. The wooden cabinets burst into flame before any part of the fire even touched them. In one minute it was much too late to save any child or adult in the room!

The sixth fire test was the one the chief had kept quiet about until the last minute. He was almost certain he knew how a fire had started in another house in the town. But a chief does not say "Arson" unless he can prove it. That is what this fire was going to do. He set it up exactly the way he thought the arsonist had set the fire two weeks before. This time, though, the alarms and detectors were removed because, if the chief's theory proved right, they would be destroyed. Also this test was no longer for testing detectors. It was testing the methods of a criminal. Some gasoline was poured on the floor and the fire was lighted. This time the temperature of the room reached 1,000° F. in only a few seconds. After that it got so hot that no thermometer could measure it. When the fire was put out, firemen checked the charred remains of the room for evidence. Next time they saw a case of arson they would recognize it.

After a fire detector detects a fire, a fire alarm is supposed to sound to warn people that a fire is starting. But some-

times, firemen warn, even a fire alarm needs to be tested. One manager of a very plush hotel in a very posh resort is still talking about what happened when he rang the alarm one morning.

A waitress had just run into the lobby from the coffee shop shouting the dreaded word "Fire!"

Instantly the manager sounded the alarm and heard the bells ringing in every corridor of the hotel. Then he called the fire department. In a few minutes firemen burst into the hotel coffee shop with hoses and foam tanks. A few tense minutes later the danger was over, and the hotel employees were relieved and happy that the fire had been controlled so quickly. Then they looked around and realized that something was missing. What was it?

A frayed electric cord caused this fire
TIMES-CHRONICLE, JENKINTOWN, PA.

"People . . . ," the manager gasped. "Where are all the hotel guests?"

The manager, firemen, and hotel security guards ran down the halls and knocked on the guests' doors. What if they had all been overcome by fumes? But that's not what had happened. They were all still sound asleep! In spite of alarms ringing in every hall, almost all the guests had slept on.

"What if the fire had spread?" argued the state's fire marshal when he heard of it. "The whole bunch of them would be dead!"

A psychologist explained what was wrong after all the hotel managers in the resort town discussed the Case of the Sleepy Guests.

"You've spent too much time making your guests feel overcomfortable here," he said. "They are surrounded by so much luxury they just can't believe there could be a fire."

Next day the fire marshal ordered testing to begin for new fire alarms to be installed in all the hotels. The alarms had to make a sound that would shake up the most relaxed guest. Everything was tested—bells, buzzers, whistles, sirens, voices. The winner was a high-pitched squeal unlike any ordinary sound. It was guaranteed to intrude on even the deepest dream. Following the unpleasant sound, though, was a voice over a loudspeaker. It was a nice, calm, loud voice telling people what to do and what not to do, because sleepy people are not always able to judge for themselves during an emergency.

34

In the last few years, testers have learned many new ways to fight fires. Only three things keep a fire burning —heat, oxygen, and fuel. Turn off any *one* of them and the fire goes out!

The first tests were to find new ways to turn off the heat in a fire. Water does not "put a fire out." What it does is to *cool* the fire so it can't burn. But even water can be improved upon. First, there are ways of using water so it can cool a fire more quickly.

One of the best ways is to use sprinklers. Before a fire can happen, many companies install sprinklers in the ceilings. Then, if there is a fire in the room, the heat sensor in the sprinkler senses the change in temperature. Suddenly dozens of showers turn on, automatically spraying cool water over the fire.

Another way to get water on a fire is with a hose. But fire hoses are heavy. A few years ago, when a fireman

An aerial boom helps firemen spray cooling water on a fire's hottest spots

TIMES-CHRONICLE, JENKINTOWN, PA.

needed to get more water onto a fire, he either had to get more hoses or find bigger ones. But now he may carry a special hose that automatically mixes water with a small amount of molecular solution that makes the water "slippery." A small hose with "slippery water" in it gets more water on the fire than an ordinary hose twice its size.

But water isn't always the best way to put out a fire. Sometimes it's the worst way! Water sprayed on a grease fire would only divide it into several small grease fires. It is equally dangerous to use water on electrical, gasoline, or combustible metals fires. These fires need dry chemicals.

There are four classes of fires and each class has a special fire extinguisher for use on that kind of fire. Class A

Workers learn how to put out a grease or oil fire with carbon dioxide

fires are fires in combustible materials such as wood, cloth, paper, rubber, and many plastics. An extinguisher with an A on a *green triangle* is for those fires only. The extinguisher with a B on a *red square* is for Class B fires—caused by flammable liquids, gases, or grease. An extinguisher marked with both an A and a B contains foam—because that puts out both kinds of fires. A Class C fire is an electrical one. It can be extinguished with the tank marked with a C on a *blue circle*. The extinguisher with a D on a *yellow star* means it is for use on fires in combustible metals like magnesium, titanium, and potassium.

A brand-new kind of dry chemical has done much to relieve this whole problem because it is marked with an A, a B, and a C. That means it puts out all three classes of fires. It is a big help to people who panic at a fire and cannot remember for the life of them which extinguisher to use on which fire! They just grab the *ABC* container.

And you can make a very good kitchen-fire extinguisher to put out grease fires. (Most kitchen fires happen around the stove.) Get a large empty coffee can and fill it with ordinary baking soda. Place it near the stove—but not behind the area where a fire might blaze up or you will not be able to reach it when you need it. If a fire starts in a pan, try to turn off the source of the heat. But do not try to move the blazing pan! Stand back and toss handfuls of the baking soda toward the base of the fire.

35

Dry chemicals (and baking soda is one) put out fires by taking away the second requirement—oxygen. The soda creates a gas (carbon dioxide) which stifles the oxygen. Of course, using baking soda is not nearly so good as having the right kind of fire extinguisher handy, but it is better than nothing.

Dry chemicals are neater than water, too. One company that puts a coating on paper has a real fire hazard because paper burns so easily. Even a small fire would cost them a great deal of money if water was used to put out the fire. All their paper supply would be ruined. So they use dry chemicals instead, and nothing gets wet.

One of the newest fire fighters that testing discovered is foam, called "light water" because it is lighter than water.

It cuts off two of the fire's needs. Not only does it cool a fire but it also cuts off some of the oxygen. An oil fire, for instance, cannot be put out with water because oil is lighter than water and it just floats on top. In fact, the oil can just travel along on a stream of water, spreading the fire farther than ever. But light water, being lighter than both water and oil, floats on top of the burning oil and covers it with a blanket of cooling foam. It has another plus, too. Light water can be mixed with salt water, or brackish water, and so it makes a good fire fighter aboard ships.

There are different kinds of foam. One oil company set its own fire to test which of two kinds of foam could put out a jet fuel fire the best. One kind put out the fire in ten minutes using 125

A new type of foam is tested on an aircraft fuel fire

gallons of foam and costing $350. The other kind put out the fire in less than two minutes using only 10 gallons and costing $50.

Another way to turn off the oxygen that a fire needs is to asphyxiate it with gas. Testers found a new kind of gas to use when they could find no other way to protect some important places from fires.

How could they protect a 107-year-old house that was filled with priceless books and antiques? Even museums can catch on fire. Another place is a vault where millions of dollars are stored. Then there is the "peaking station" of an electric company where emergency generators are stored. A fire in that spot would cause a complete blackout in a large city and there would be no hope for any emergency power. In places like these it would be impossible to use water to put out a fire. Even dry chemicals would leave behind a mess that might cause as much trouble as the fire. What else was there?

Halogen gas had been around for many years, but it had a terrible reputation. Some of its relatives were dangerous. They helped put out fires, but a few times they had killed the people who were using them. When a new kind of halogen, called Halon 1301, appeared to be much better behaved, it had to pass many stiff tests before it could prove itself. It could be used safely for those types of very special places because it was not so dangerous for people. And it could be used to put out three kinds of fires—*A, B,* and *C.*

When a spark from the living room fireplace landed on his new carpet, the owner of this home learned too late that the rug was flammable
TIMES-CHRONICLE, JENKINTOWN, PA.

The third way to stop fires is to take away their fuel. This is one project that testers go all out for. If the fuel material can be made so it won't burn, many fires can be nipped in the bud.

Clothing that won't burn is a start. After the Apollo space capsule fire, NASA tested 5,000 new materials. Only 3 rated high enough because astronauts—and aquanauts too—work in an atmosphere where there is a high amount of oxygen. But many of the materials NASA could not use are perfect for other purposes. They are made into work clothes for people who work where there is a high risk of fire— around a racetrack pit, for example. Some of the materials are made into protective blankets for both drivers and

37

pit crew in case of a flash fire. Some are made into flight suits for pilots and into hospital pajamas for patients confined to bed.

But until recently, children under five years of age—the most likely people in the world to play with matches and get burned—had only dangerous clothing to wear. A pair of children's pajamas could burn in a few seconds. A fuzzy pair of cowboy chaps could flare up if a cigarette touched them. Now a new law states that the makers of children's sleepwear must tell people whether their pajamas are flammable or fire-resistant. But for other clothes, parents still cannot be sure which are the safest.

There is a way to make your own cotton Halloween costume or holiday decorations fire-resistant. You can treat cotton camping items, too. The flame-retardant treatment is good for items not washed often, since washing removes the flameproofing. The two products used to make the solution are dangerous if swallowed, so keep the mixture away from younger brothers and sisters.

Buy a box of borax at the supermarket and some boric acid at a drugstore. Mix 1 cup of borax with ½ cup of boric acid. Stir together with 8 cups (2 quarts) of hot water. The cotton garment you want to make flame-retardant (which is not necessarily flame-*proof*) must be dry when you dip it into the solution. Make sure it gets completely wet with the solution. Then squeeze out the extra water and either

38

A hot test for an astronaut's suit

NASA

drip-dry or put into a clothes dryer.

A few things to remember: this works only on cotton. Do not wear the material next to your skin if you have any open sores or abrasions. Do not use the solution on a baby's diapers. Store the flame-retardant solution out of reach. And remember, the treatment works only until the garment is washed again.

[PHOTOS OPPOSITE]
(Top photo) *What appears to be a white rounded building is part of an airplane. Half is protected by a coating of foam. The other half is not protected*

(Middle photo) *5,000 gallons of fuel are set on fire*

(Bottom) *The half that was not covered by foam was gone within two minutes*

AVCO CORP.

Another fire fuel is the furnishings inside a house. Some people cannot live with their rugs. Often they don't know that until it's too late. Someone drops a cigarette or a hot iron, or a spark from the fireplace ignites the rug. The Good Housekeeping Institute tested 5,000 rugs to see which were flammable.

A piece of carpet to be tested is cut into 9-inch squares. First these are put into a warm oven to be dried out— just as carpet in a house dries out from the heat. Then the pieces are cooled. Each piece of carpet is put into a small frame so that only a circle about 8 inches across can be seen. A small "burning" pill is placed in the center of the circle and lighted with a match. It takes the pill less than two minutes to burn. For a carpet to pass the test with honors, the only burned place should be the spot where the pill was. The carpet can still pass if it burned only a little distance around the center. But if it burned to within an inch of the circle's outside edge, it flunked and is not safe to use in a house.

Wood has always been one of the best fuels for a fire. Now fires cannot even depend on wood, since testers have found ways to make wood less flammable. At a lumberyard, a builder can find wood marked "slow-burning" and "fire-retardant," and even "incombustible." Those pieces of wood have just passed some strict tests. The standards for those tests are the same whether the wood is tested in Wiscon-

40

sin or in Georgia. The wood is placed on a frame in a room without drafts and a gas flame is lighted underneath. If, after forty minutes with the gas flame touching the wood, there are no flames and the wood glows only where the fire touched it, that piece of wood can be labeled "incombustible." If there are just short, occasional flames that do not last longer than two minutes after the gas flame is removed, the wood is fire-retardant. If the flaming afterward lasts five minutes, it is called "slow-burning" wood. But woods that don't pass these tests are all listed as "combustible," which means they burn.

Most paints have an oil base and these make great fuel for a fire. But now, in place of ordinary paint, a piece of wood—or metal, plastic, plaster, or concrete—can have a fire-retardant coating. Such coatings are called intumescent, or swollen, coatings because when they are subjected to heat such as that of a fire, they swell up to 150 or 200 times their original thickness. They bubble up so much that the fire cannot burn, because it can no longer get near the wood underneath the coating.

The testers found a piece of Douglas fir, which has a high flame-spread rating, to test the new intumescent paint. One piece of Douglas fir, without any paint, was used for comparison. Then an acetylene torch (3,000° F.) was held over the wood with the coating. Instantly the coating swelled up, insulating the wood underneath it. After the burning, the bubbled-up paint was scraped off and the wood underneath was found to be as good as new.

Making tests with the new coating, researchers found another use for it. They painted a bomb with it. Then they started a fire. Ordinarily the bomb would have burst within thirty seconds. But with the coating on it reflecting the heat from the fire, the bomb lasted nine minutes—perhaps long enough for putting out the fire and preventing a huge catastrophe.

The same sort of heat-resistant coating was used to make the ablative heat shield that brought the Apollo space capsules safely back into the earth's atmosphere. People had said that even if man ever managed to get out of the earth's atmosphere, he could never survive the reentry without burning up. Thanks to a heat shield only 2 inches thick, those people were wrong. The shield actually burned and formed a char barrier which kept everything behind it cool. The inside of the space capsule became only 10° warmer. The outside heated up from 150° F. to 5,500° F.

There have been plane crashes that people might have survived if only they could have waited for the fire trucks. In six minutes fire trucks can be at the side of a plane that crashes during takeoff or landing. In another two minutes they can put out the fire from the spilled gasoline that surrounds the plane. But in less than two minutes the heat from the fire has killed the passengers.

The company that made the space capsule's heat shield decided to do some testing. The testers took a large C-47 fuselage and divided it in half. One half was protected only as much as most airplanes. But the other half was protected with insulating foam and intumescent coating. Then they set fire to 5,000 gallons of jet fuel.

Remote-control movie cameras recorded the inside temperatures of both airplane sections. In one and three-fourths minutes, the passengers in the unprotected half would have been dead from the heat. But those in the protected section would have had twelve minutes—more than enough time to get the fire trucks there and put out the fire. There were no gas fumes and the heat was about like that of a sauna bath.

Every test brings scientists a little closer to their goal of controlling fire. At least they understand it much better than they did in the days before testing with fire.

3

Testing with water

DROWN IT

A SCIENTIST may think he knows everything there is to know about a product. Then he adds some water—and discovers he didn't know everything after all. That's why many tests have to include testing with water.

One company had some bales of wool sitting on a train platform waiting for a train. There were so many that they were piled all around the little train station. Unfortunately, before the train arrived it began to rain hard. It rained so heavily there were floods in the low areas, and it was four days before the train could reach the station. Meanwhile, the bales of wool were soaking up water and swelling to almost twice their size. Some leaned against the station wall and knocked a portion of it down. Others leaned against two posts holding up a part of the platform roof and the posts collapsed. The trainmen could not lift the heavy bales, so they had to be unwrapped and dried out. The station was a shambles before the week was over.

Another company discovered that water can start fires. Some chemicals had been packed in containers that were not waterproof. These were inside a freight car, but the roof leaked and water poured onto the cardboard containers. Suddenly the chemicals burst into flames.

Finding just the right kind of container can take a lot of testing. When the Romans conquered the Celts, they thought they had beaten some stupid barbarians. But they were surprised to find that the Celts had invented some very convenient containers—better than any the Romans had. We call them barrels, but the Romans had never seen such things. They promptly stole the idea. Barrels were watertight and hard to break. For centuries they have been the only way to ship foods, liquids, and many other items.

But barrels are heavy and expensive to handle. Besides, they are not a very handy shape for storing because of the bulge in the center that gives them their strength. The bulge makes them take up more space than they should. Steel drums, a newer invention, have straight sides, but they are too heavy. A very

42

good kind of drum was made of fiberboard—until one day a shipment of fiber drums was left out in the rain.

"Find some way to build a weatherproof fiber drum that we can store outdoors," said a note received by a company's research department one day. Instantly every engineer got to work. They never knew there were so many kinds of glue or so many ways to wind layers of fiberboard. Each time they tested their new containers in an environmental chamber, and most of them collapsed. Four inches of water—the equivalent of a huge storm—poured down on the drums every hour for several weeks. Those that survived were left outdoors in snow, sleet, and the worst of humid tropics. Some were filled with salt, because salt absorbs moisture. (Everyone knows how salt clogs up the saltshaker when the weather is humid.) At long last, one of the fiberboard drums, put together with a new kind of glue, outlasted all

Will a jetliner's tires skid in pouring rain, sleet, or snow? This tester finds out
GOODYEAR TIRE & RUBBER CO.

the others. After the test the salt inside still poured freely. The old Celts' barrel finally has a rival.

Some testing laboratories specialize in "environmental testing." That means testing things in some of the extreme environments that nature provides. If a photographer wants to take pictures in the jungles of Panama for a travel magazine, he should be sure his camera and film case have been tested for that environment—the humidity of the jungle and the almost continuous rain in parts of the country.

Even a raincoat gets environmental tests. When its label says it is "waterproof" and "a windbreaker," testers make sure it really is. One of the testers puts on the coat and goes into a "climatology room." There he walks on

After 2 days in "rain," three of the four fiber drums collapse and the wood stacked on top of them topples
CONTINENTAL CAN CO.

43

a treadmill while another tester, staying nice and dry outside the glassed-in room, arranges an electronic storm by computer. The wind blows and the rain turns from mist to downpour. Since the tester is moving on a treadmill, he can also test whether the raincoat has enough buttons on it or whether the wind blows the coat open and allows the rain to soak his clothes underneath. In the same room, the humidity can range from jungle steam to the driest

Dishwasher performance is evaluated with an egg-and-spinach smear

desert or from 120° F. to 10° below zero.

Automobile-proving grounds always include some sort of environmental testing. When a car drives through a deep puddle, a "gone" feeling for the driver can sometimes result. What's gone is the brakes. Until they dry out, the car may be almost without braking power. To learn whether the new automobile design handles well in bad rainstorms, the driver detours through some deep water. At the same time he checks the electrical system and any leaks in the body of the car.

Water is supposed to clean things—or that is what dishwasher and washing machine manufacturers thought until they found out that it's not necessarily so. Careful housekeepers would be shocked at the sight of a dishwasher-

A wet detour tests a new car for leaks, bad brakes, and splashes that get in the engine

testing lab. Most manufacturers claim that their dishwashers will do a perfect job on dirty dishes that are not even rinsed off first. Is that true? The testers at Good Housekeeping Institute want to find out before they allow such an advertisement to appear in their magazine. The testers at Consumers Union also plan to test dishwashers to find out which are the best.

The Good Housekeeping recipe for dishwasher mess includes a can of drained spinach and a can of green beans with juice. This is mixed in a blender with some mayonnaise, vege-

Making stains on pieces of material is a good way to compare effectiveness of different detergents and cleaning aids

table shortening, and green food coloring. The gooey stuff is smeared on forks, plates, and cups. Then it sits around for an hour or so getting hard before going into the dishwasher.

A slightly different treat is waiting for the dishwashers tested by the Consumers Union. Their glasses show traces of milk, tomato juice, and orange juice. The cups are stained with coffee. Dishes and utensils show evidence that at least twenty kinds of food were sampled. There are bits of beef stew, spaghetti, vegetables, peanut butter, cheese spread, oatmeal, and soft-boiled egg yolk on everything.

When the Good Housekeeping Institute tests a clothes washer, it uses a good test that you can try at home. Tear a large rag into strips about 6 inches wide. Write on the strips about 4 inches apart the names of the stains you are going to test. Be sure to use a waterproof ink! Beneath each name, put a good-size smear of that stain. Then try washing the strips in your own washing machine. See what comes out and what stays. You may want to try other strips of the same stains to see whether the soap, detergent, water temperature, or bleach makes any difference.

A fishing line was tested for strength before it was sold. But after the line was used in the water, it appeared that more tests were needed.

The whole point in fishing is for the fish to think that the bait dangling before his hungry eyes has no strings attached. Fishermen try to make sure that the leader, the piece between the fishing line and the baited hook, is as invisible as possible. Some even tried dyeing their fishing line the same color as the water. But the result usually was that the fish could see the line, while the fisherman couldn't see it at all.

A diver-photographer goes down for a fisheye view of the invisible line

The line is clearly visible to the fisherman's view

Then the DuPont Company decided to look at the whole subject from a fish's eye view—as well as from the fisherman's. The fisherman needs to see his line so he can guide a hooked fish away from weeds or half-submerged logs, but the fish should not see it at all —not even so much as the knot used to tie on the hook. To try some new kinds of fishing line, DuPont sent human fish—in scuba gear—down under the water.

One of the lines was a very special kind. It was nylon, with a fluorescent chemical added. Above the water, where there is ultraviolet light in daytime, the line shows up clearly. Just under the surface, before all the ultraviolet light is filtered out, the line glows as it does above the water. But to a fish, the light-blue color of the line blends in with the color of the water and sky above. Farther down, as the scuba divers reported, the ultraviolet light is filtered out by the deep water and the line is invisible.

Recently some scientists who like fishing found that another kind of testing was needed if they were ever to catch any fish at all. The best fishing is usually where there are reefs or at least some protected spots where the small fish can hide. Some areas have no rocks, pilings, reefs, or any places that attract fish. (The Gulf of Mexico is noted for its smooth bottom.) A tire manufacturer had suggested that a fairly good reef might be made with old, worn-out tires. Not many people paid attention to his suggestion at first,

*At end of 2-year test, this tire has almost
become a part of an underwater reef*

GOODYEAR TIRE & RUBBER CO.

but after a while it began to sound like
a crazy idea that just might work!

Several tires are bundled together in
a special machine, weighted with concrete and anchored on the ocean floor.
Most of the tire reefs are 20 feet deep,
although they are different lengths.
Testing includes monitoring by scientists from a marine ecology station to
decide the best depth and size for the
man-made reefs. Tires that have been
under the water for only a year no
longer look like tires. They are so covered with barnacles that already they
look like the real thing. Evidently the
fish think so too.

Water, in the form of 40-foot waves,
spoiled a different test along the California coast recently. Engineers had

*Engineers test the breaking point of a
giant concrete shape modeled on a child's
toy*

*Found to be much stronger than square
blocks, the new shapes are used to build
a jetty*

U.S. ARMY CORPS OF ENGINEERS

47

just finished building a strong new jetty with solid concrete blocks that weighed 100 tons each.

After the storm had ruined the jetty, the Army Corps of Engineers began searching for new ways to build jetties. A tougher material—concrete with steel fibers mixed in it—had already been put to use. But they were not sure whether a solid square block of concrete was the best shape to use. They literally searched the world for a better shape. They found it in a South African toy box!

Long ago, South African children played a game using the small ankle bones of a goat. One bone is called a *dolos;* the plural is *dolosse.* These look like the jacks that children play with in this country. A South African engineer had used small *dolosse* to build a jetty in his own country. Even though the new shape, cast in plain concrete, had worked so well, he did not patent his idea, because he wanted others to be able to use it.

When the Army Engineers in California decided to try building with *dolosse,* they knew theirs would have to be very much larger. They tested the strange-looking shapes every way they could think of—dropping them down on one fluke, pushing the flukes apart. But every time, the *dolosse* showed their strength. Although each one weighed less than half the weight of the old square block, it was much stronger.

Finally the engineers were ready to build two new jetties, using almost 5,000 giant-size models of goat ankle

48

Divers' watches are tested to be sure they work at depths of 700 feet
BULOVA WATCH CO., INC.

bones. Much of the strength of the jetties was in the way the *dolosse* were fitted together. A specially built crane lifted each one into its place. The crane operator carefully checked off each *dolos* he placed, because each had to fit against the next and face the sea.

Testing under the sea adds a new element to testing with water, whether the tests are on wristwatches or on submarines. For centuries men had tried to dive under the sea in boats and live long enough to get back to tell others what they had seen. More often than not, the water pressure under the sea was much more than any of them had expected.

Robert Fulton had been a young boy when a turtle-shaped submarine had tried to sink a British ship during the American Revolution. But that had been only partly a submarine. It did not even submerge completely. Now Fulton's "plunging boat," the *Nautilus,* was ready for its first test on July 29, 1800.

A few people stood along the shoreline in the cool breeze that rippled the water outside the French harbor. The watchers were almost certain they had come to see three foolhardy men die. Yet they could not help being impressed by the confidence of the young American inventor, Robert Fulton.

Until that day, Fulton's *Nautilus* had existed only on paper. The inventor had tried to talk Napoleon into building a "plunging boat" to sink the British warships that were blockading French ports. The *Nautilus,* he told Napoleon, could plant a bomb under a ship's hull and escape before it blew up. Then France would rule the seas. But Napoleon wasn't buying.

Fulton was sure that Napoleon would feel different after the test. The boat the French audience saw looked just like a sailboat, but suddenly the three men sailing it leaped from their seats. One furled the sail, another folded back the mast so it fit tight to the deck, and the third opened a hatch. Soon all three men disappeared below and, while one closed the hatch cover, two began cranking an endless belt. The propellers turned and the boat began to move forward. Ballast tanks

filled with water, and gradually the boat disappeared beneath the waves.

Below decks, the two men turning the cranks pumped away. Two candles gave them a little light. At least, they thought, as long as the candles burned they knew there was air to breathe. The boat went 25 feet under the water. But would it go back up again? Two of the men were not so sure. (The third man was Fulton.) The next five minutes were the longest in their lives. Fulton had not always been right. There was that steamboat he had built on the Seine River. It had looked very good, too—until his men carried the machinery onto the boat and it had sunk straight to the bottom of the river.

At last Fulton gave the order for the submarine to go up again. It worked! When they opened the hatch and gasped the sweet, fresh air the men noticed that the river current had carried them far from the watching crowd. Once more Fulton ordered a dive. This time they stayed down seventeen minutes. But the current was so swift that they could not steer the little boat. Fulton would have to make some improvements before he tried sinking any British ships.

The big test was almost a year later. This time instead of candles two windows provided light inside the sub. And bottles of compressed air made it possible to keep the *Nautilus* submerged for six hours. But the part of the test that Napoleon's officers had come to see was still ahead.

Slowly the submarine crept toward

49

a 40-foot ship that had been anchored in the harbor for the test. The tiny *Nautilus* attached a bomb to the ship's underside and moved as far away as possible in the short time before the bomb exploded. Suddenly a blast ripped the ship to shreds. The crowd on the shore cheered excitedly. The submarine was safe.

"There was nothing left but the buoy and cable," said Fulton in a letter. But Napoleon did not buy on that day either.

The British were impressed, however. Within a few weeks (news did not travel fast in those days), they had sent secret messages to every ship captain in their Navy to be on the lookout for Fulton's submarine. Then they sent a man to find Fulton and persuade him to come to England "to talk business." Fulton decided that since the French didn't want his idea, he might as well sell it to the other side. Actually the British had no intention of buying it either. They already ruled the sea. But they wanted to be very sure that the French never built submarines. Nine years after his first dream of boats moving under the sea, Fulton gave up and sailed for America. Almost immediately he began work on the invention that finally brought him fame—his steamboat.

Today submarines can stay underwater for months at a time. Scientists are beginning to test the undersea world with much more in mind than just a highway for submarines. With so much pollution on land, many people feel that the future of our world may lie under the sea. Someday that world may supply fuel, food, clothing, perhaps even living space.

The U.S. Navy has been experimenting for many years with ideas for living and building on the bottom of the ocean. When men build on land they have all sorts of technology to help them—a good power supply, pickup trucks, ways to dig solid foundations, cranes, bulldozers to move what's in the way, hydraulic tools like chain saws and pumps. Now the Navy is testing these same machines underwater. "Seacon" is the name for this sea floor construction test project.

The new inventions are divided into two groups. Some inventions are for very deep water where divers in scuba gear cannot go. Others are for shallower waters where the divers can work comfortably beside their machines.

The spot on the ocean floor chosen for the tests is probably one of the best-known places in the ocean. For months, cores had been taken to see what kind of ground lay beneath the sea floor. Underwater cameras had recorded the movements on the bottom —the shifting sands and currents. A capsule-shaped structure, attached to a concrete foundation, had been installed on the bottom. It was the center for the rest of the tests. In it were all the instruments needed to monitor the ocean floor for a year. The gauges inside the capsule were monitored by men on land via closed-circuit television cameras placed inside the capsule. Even the shape of the capsule was a test, because the Navy engineers think it may be the best shape for the undersea houses they will build someday.

Machines tested in deep water must be remote-controlled because they go too far down for men to dive. But there will be times when a "foreman" or the "architect" will want to go down to see how the digging is coming along. For this purpose, there is an experimental observatory built to hold two people. Its acrylic hull gives them an all-the-way-around view. One of the new machines is an underwater excavator— like a steam shovel on land. Another is called Dotipos—short for Deep Ocean Test-in-Place Observation System. The operator of Dotipos sits above in a ship and sees what he is doing via a television screen. He can collect samples off the bottom, drill 10-foot long cores from the sea floor, and move heavy objects wherever he wants.

Divers in scuba gear help do the testing of the new inventions that work in shallower water. Almost everything a construction worker has onshore he can have in the water, too. First there are special electrohydraulic tools that

Seacon's undersea lab is tested in water before being lowered 600 feet to the ocean floor

U.S. NAVY

can be used safely in the ocean. The worker may have to learn a few new techniques, though. For example, if he wants to use an underwater electric drill, he will have to fasten himself to the wall because the drill will keep pushing him backward.

The pickup truck that carries a worker and his tools on land has its twin under the sea, too. It's called the CAV (Construction Assistance Vehicle) and can carry cargo, tools, and workers to their underwater construction site. It even provides a place for them to plug in their electrohydraulic tools. The CAV cruises slowly, at about 2.5 knots or almost 3 mph, down to 120 feet below the surface.

On land a forklift carries heavy loads around a building site and hoists them up wherever the operator wants them. Undersea, the BTV (Buoyancy Transport Vehicle) does the job. It can carry 1,000 pounds around. If a ship should drop its 500-pound anchor in a spot where it isn't going to hold, the BTV, with a diver directing it, could easily lift the anchor and move it.

When wind on land blows the dust so workers can't see what they're doing, the dust can be sprayed with water to make it settle down. But what happens under the ocean when the currents stir up the bottom sediment so divers can't see what they're doing? They call in a CAV. It skims slowly over the ocean floor, laying behind it a heavy film of plastic. Or what happens when divers have to work in icy-cold water? Testers are still trying to

52

Divers have the same problems that men in space have using power tools—the men must be fastened tight or the force of the tool will push them backward

U.S. NAVY

find ways to heat suits, either chemically or some other way, to keep divers comfortable.

While Navy researchers are testing new ways to conquer the sea's strange environment, other researchers are trying to probe more of the sea's riddles.

Benjamin Franklin was one man who could never stand a mystery. And one puzzle that had bothered him for some time was the Gulf Stream. Was it a river in the sea? Where did it come from? One day in 1768 another question added to the mystery.

As postmaster general, Franklin had kept busy trying to increase the speed of mail deliveries. Why was it, someone asked, that it took American fishermen two weeks *less* to cross the Atlantic Ocean than it took British merchant ships? The British actually had faster ships. It just didn't make sense.

It didn't to Franklin either. He asked his cousin, who was captain of a Nantucket Island whaling ship. The answer was really no mystery at all, explained Timothy Folger. Whalers had always followed the edges of the Gulf Stream because that was where they caught the most whales. They knew the boundaries of the warm stream so well they could draw charts of it. The whaling ships made use of the fast stream when they sailed toward England. But coming home, the fishermen avoided the strong current because it was a one-way road. When they had to cross it, they did so by the shortest route. But for some reason, British ships always sailed in the Gulf Stream, even though it meant bucking the strong current almost the whole way back to America.

Franklin had his cousin mark the Gulf Stream for him on a chart. Then he printed enough maps for every ship captain to have one. But the British captains did not take quickly to change. They were afraid of running into shoals if they tried to leave the Stream.

Today the Gulf Stream is still mys-

The pick-up truck is as necessary under the sea as it is on the land. Divers take the CAV for its first tests

The underwater forklift can carry up to 1,000 pounds for the undersea construction worker

terious. Scientists recently decided to test a new kind of submarine that would in turn test the Gulf Stream.

To help plan the voyage and design the submarine, the scientists went to Switzerland for Jacques Piccard, a famous oceanographer who had studied the undersea world from a bathyscaph in the Mediterranean. They told him of their plans to "drift" through the Gulf Stream in a submarine that would be designed to stay at certain depths. The sub would have several windows so that the crew could watch the sea life in the warm stream. Piccard was to keep records of the trip, and later write a book about it.

Unlike Fulton's submarine that was not tested until it was finished, the *Ben Franklin* was tested at every step along the way. The U.S. Navy insisted on most of the tests because they planned to send some of their men on the trip.

And, unless the sub passed all their rigid tests, the Navy would not allow their men to enter it. The rest of the crew were rather glad the Navy felt that way. By the time the *Ben Franklin* was christened, its builders had a manual filled with standards that had been set during the building. Every research sub built since that day will have to conform to those standards.

While engineers planned serious tests —like the hull strength test with strain gauges on both the inside and the outside of the hull—the *Ben Franklin*'s crew tried a test of their own. They built a house with a deck of cards on one of the tables. The sub passed their test when it moved forward under the water—and the house of cards didn't collapse.

Finally the last day of tests came. After a three-day cruise in the Gulf Stream with everything running smoothly, the crew got the word that they could continue for the next month. Above them, on the surface of the water, was the contact ship that was to stay with them constantly. They had radio contact, but because the radio used up the batteries, this contact was kept to a bare minimum—after the first conversation when the man who was cooking for the crew suddenly needed to make a radio call: "Quick," he said, "how many cups are in a pint?"

For most of the time, the *Ben Franklin* drifted at about 200 meters (about 650 feet) below the surface. Because the sub was noiseless and because it moved at about the same rate of speed

The Ben Franklin, *built to test the Gulf Stream, on precruise checkout tests*

GRUMMAN AEROSPACE CORP.

as the surrounding water, fish seemed completely unafraid of it. In fact, the crew would have been happier if one swordfish had been a little less' courageous. He charged one of the windows so hard they half expected to see his sword come through the porthole. Fortunately he didn't make another try for it.

During its 1500-mile trip through the Gulf Stream, the little *Ben Franklin* did not answer all the questions of the scientists. Sometimes the sub swung back and forth gently like a pendulum. Occasionally it even turned around and drifted backward. Once, for no apparent reason, it got caught in a current of water that sent it quickly out of the warm stream and into the cold ocean itself. At other times it seemed to get caught in gigantic undersea waves.

Once it rode 65 meters (about 213 feet) up one side of a wave and down the other side 50 meters (about 164 feet).

The men on the contact ship riding the Gulf Stream above the *Ben Franklin* were just as puzzled. They had to ride the 1500 miles backward! If they had coasted with the current, they would have lost the sub very quickly, because the water moved much faster on the surface than down below. So they had to point the bow into the current and use the motor to slow down enough to stay with the sub.

Although many scientists thought they already knew quite a lot about the Gulf Stream, the *Ben Franklin* showed them that the Stream still holds many surprises. This was only the first of many tests to come.

55

4

Destructive testing

SMASH IT

Tests are usually made to find out just how strong a material is. But sometimes that is not enough. There are times when testers need to know exactly when something has reached the breaking point. That's when they test to destruction.

Dionysius the Elder was the first dictator to wear an iron vest because, as is usual with dictators, he had more enemies than friends. He ruled the largest city in the ancient Greek world in 399 B.C. At first, destruction was a hobby with him, but he became so good at it that it was soon his chief occupation.

He gathered the most skilled workmen from every city—even from cities that were still his enemies—by paying huge wages plus bonuses for the most destructive ideas of the year. His research teams came through with many new weapons, but one of their best efforts was the catapult. This was like a giant-sized crossbow mounted on a pedestal and it could shoot arrows 6 feet long. Tests were held in secret until the right day should come for the world to hear about the weapon.

Two years after the catapult's invention, Dionysius decided it was time to get the last of the Carthaginians out of Sicily, which was then part of the Greek world, and back to Carthage, where they belonged. The people of Motya, the Carthaginian colony, were not worried. They had spotted the Greek ships coming and had already sent for help. Himilkon, their hero, would soon arrive with his fleet of warships from Carthage and would send the Greeks scurrying for cover.

But it did not work out that way. When Himilkon arrived, Dionysius had set up his catapults with every one aimed at the fleet from Carthage. The Carthaginians could not even come near the Greek ships because the barrage was so powerful. Himilkon finally turned his ships around and left the Motyans to defend themselves as best they could. In a few hours, the catapults had destroyed the city walls and a new kind of war—with artillery—had begun. Never again would wars be just man against man with victory going to the strongest.

56

Meanwhile, the secret of the catapult was out and Dionysius was taking no chances on being beaten by others using his own invention. He knew it was only a matter of time before one of his enemies would figure it out and come after him with a catapult. Actually, it was many years, but the dictator had no way of knowing that he would have so long to prepare. He began testing his own defenses, turning one of his catapults toward his own gate to test how well it withstood a bombardment like the one he had given the Motyans. Destructive testing had begun.

Dionysius would probably have enjoyed seeing how some scientists recently tried to solve a problem that miners and tunnel-builders face when they suddenly reach hard rock. There are all sorts of drills and machines to burrow through most rock. But where the rock is very hard, the boring chews up the toughest drill. Men might spend days hacking their way through only a few feet of rock.

Then scientists remembered that there is enough energy contained in a

An old army 105 mm cannon aims at its peacetime target—a section of hard rock. Holes have been drilled to outline the tunnel's shape

At the moment of impact, a fireball lights up the excavation

The new tunnel is now 13 feet high and extends 22 feet into the mountain
PHYSICS INTERNATIONAL

gun to break up rock. Why not try a gun? They bought a few old cannons and armed them with concrete "bullets" a foot long. Aiming the cannons toward the hard-rock face, they fired. It worked! The first tests destroyed the rock better than any drills yet invented —and there are plenty of old cannons around.

There are plenty of explosives, too, and the Army Corps of Engineers has been testing ways to put them to good use. "Cratering" is placing a crater, or hole, where it is needed. Nature can often be improved upon by cratering.

Widening a ship channel so ships will not run aground is usually not a hard job. But when that channel is in Alaska, where the water current is almost as swift as a waterfall and the channel bottom is of solid granite, then widening the channel is a super-sized job. The Army Engineers are usually invited to do that sort of work, and they use cratering.

Instant harbors are another use for the new cratering technique. The Army Engineers were called in to make two destructive tests that would help improve local ecology. One was planned for a reservoir in pock-marked Montana country. Three tiny lakes were near the reservoir's edge, but rocky ground separated them from each other. In a matter of years, they would all dry up. But if they could be joined, and connected with the constant fresh-water supply of the reservoir, they would form a long harbor. The shallower, more protected water would be

58

When engineers tried cratering in coral, the crushed coral came down as finely ground sand

U.S. ARMY CORPS OF ENGINEERS

a perfect place for fish to hatch their young. The experiment was successful. After craters were blasted between the lakes and another hole was blasted between the last lake and the reservoir, the water poured in to form a long finger of protected water.

For the second test, engineers tried the new cratering technique in Hawaii. The hard rock they had to remove was coral. They had expected to make a large crater, such as they had made when they tried the technique on land. But this time it was different. When the blast went off, the coral was crushed and all the water squeezed out of it. The coral blew 1,000 feet into the sky and came down—as fine sand.

These new tests will all be important when the day comes to do something about the Panama Canal. Already ships are too large to go through it easily. In some places, only three feet of space is left on either side of big ships, and supertankers cannot go through the Canal at all. Either the Canal must be made larger or a new one must be built somewhere else. Engineers will have to do a great deal of testing before any country will allow explosives, especially nuclear ones, to be used to build a new canal.

When testers start smashing products, they have to have good reasons, because destructive testing costs money. One of the best reasons is to save lives. Researchers who study auto accidents find that certain types of accidents happen over and over again—and that many of those accidents should not be killing people.

Highway police were getting discouraged because one particular corner seemed to be causing many more accidents than any other place along a certain expressway. For some reason, drivers often misjudged the curve and slid off the road when it was icy or even wet. If drivers only knew they were coming to a dangerous place, they would certainly be more careful there.

The driver of this car would have been killed, if he had not hit one of the new "breakaway" signs

"Why don't we put a sign there to warn people?" someone suggested.

But the accidents did not stop after the sign was put up. Instead, cars skidded off the road and ran into the sign, making the accidents even more deadly than before. Other signs along the highway were also being hit, even though researchers had tested various kinds of paint on their supports to make them stand out against the background and so be easy to see. Express-

ways, where traffic moves too fast for drivers to notice interchanges without signs to warn them, have to have some sort of signs. The signs cannot hang on skyhooks. What can be done?

Researchers decided to try making signs that could not hurt people. At first they thought of constructing them of softer material—but plastic signs blew over in the wind. After many tests, scientists finally made a sign that could stand up to the worst of winter storms, summer hails, vandals who tried to steal it, and even cars that bumped into it lightly. Yet the same sign, when hit by a car moving fast enough to have an accident, would snap off and fall harmlessly to one side.

Auto crashes kill more young people today than all other causes put together. That is why the United States Government joined with several other countries to sponsor a search that included many destructive tests.

It all began with a contest. The United States was to build the "world's safest heavy family car." European auto companies were to come up with the "world's safest intermediate-sized cars" and Japanese companies were to build the "world's safest compact cars." Crashes were heard around the world as each country put their "best" cars to the tests. After the dust settled, they would all compare notes and share their best ideas.

Meanwhile, in this country automobile companies began reading the rules of the contest. One rule was that the passengers in the winning cars had to be still alive after several kinds of crashes. Since the passengers were all dummies, this meant that delicate instruments inside their bodies would decide whether they were alive or dead. (Some were actually classified as being only "slightly killed"!) Another rule was that the passengers had to be alive in spite of themselves. Safety belts and shoulder harnesses are excellent, but people "forget" to use them. These passengers had to be "passively restrained." That means the seat belts, or whatever protected them, had to fasten by themselves.

Any company could enter the contest, but each had to build at least six cars. From the sounds of the tests, there would not be much left of any of the cars at the end. The cars would be called ESV's—Experimental Safety Vehicles. Each of them would cost several thousand dollars, because they had to be custom-made.

The nondestructive tests were all made first. Then the tests got rougher and tougher. For the destructive tests, the engineers studied the worst accidents that happen most often. Of the six ESV's made by each company, four were tested in serious accidents.

When one car has a head-on collision with another going the same speed, the impact is just the same as if the car had driven off the roof of a seven-story building and landed in the street below! To find out what would have happened to ESV #1 and its passengers, the testers smashed it while traveling at 50 mph into a solid wall. Instru-

60

Experimental Safety Vehicle # 1 before and after a crash test

U.S. DEPT. OF TRANSPORTATION, NHTSA

ments inside the dummy showed that the front seat passenger hit the windshield with the force of more than a ton.

What happens when a driver runs through a red light and meets another car at the intersection? This test was tried by ESV #2 to find out. When one driver stops suddenly and the driver in the car behind is not paying attention, there is a hard rear-end collision—the fate of ESV #3. The fourth car tested what happens when the driver skids off the highway and rolls over at 70 mph. Few humans ever survive this kind of accident, but to pass the test the dummy occupants of the ESV had to survive. Not much was left of the four ESV's after these tests, but their passengers were "alive." And when the same tests were tried on ordinary cars —the kinds we are driving every day— the testers could see how very much better all the ESV's were.

People will never be able to buy a car just like one of the ESV's, but cars of the future may borrow many of the experimental features that performed well during the tests. Some of these new features may appear very soon. A periscope rearview mirror that shows the whole roadway behind—as well as a car passing—is popular with drivers. Bumpers that collapse and absorb some of the impact can save many lives. But some of the ESV features are so restricting that most people will not want them even if they do save lives. One is a padded barricade that fits against the chests of passengers riding in the backseat. They cannot cross their ankles, read a book, eat a candy bar, or look out of the window until the rear door is opened and the barricade lifted! Another safety feature is to have no windows that open. The driver has a tiny window just big enough for him to reach out and pay his turnpike toll. The

61

How does the tester know airbags will not inflate at the wrong time? (Top) Test driver zooms up ramp at 45 mph. Hub cap falls off when car is 5½ feet in air— seen under left front wheel

(Middle) Car lands on road with force of 26 G's

(Bottom) The airbag does not open because the car did not have a front-end collision

ALLSTATE INSURANCE COMPANIES

62

passengers have to rely on an air conditioner to be able to breathe.

One of the safety features that may be used in the future is airbags. They are supposed to open only when there is a crash from the front of the car. At other times, the airbags are hidden out of the way. In the fraction of a second after an impact—before the passenger's head has had a chance to hit the windshield—the airbag inflates. Then it deflates in half a second so the passenger can get out of the car.

When airbags were first suggested, people did not like the idea. What if the bag inflated when the driver least expected it? It might cause a wreck. The makers of airbags have done a great deal of improving and testing. They have even destroyed cars to show that airbags will inflate only when they are meant to—not when they shouldn't.

The most dangerous place to be during an accident has always been near the windshield. In the old days, the windshield glass shattered and showered people with sharp splinters. Many lives were saved after safety glass was invented and installed in every window

[PHOTOS OPPOSITE]
Testers crash another car to show the airbag will work when it should (Top) The airbag inflates so quickly after collision starts that passenger's head cannot hit windshield (Middle) In less than ½ a second, airbag deflates again, so passenger can escape (Bottom) Passenger leaves by window to protect test instruments in car
ALLSTATE INSURANCE COMPANIES

(Top) *A passenger would have gone head-first through this windshield in a car made before 1966*

(Bottom) *The same ball (used to simulate a person's head) hits the new type of windshield twice as hard, but the glass stretches*

of a car. But still, in an accident, a passenger's head can go through even a windshield of safety glass.

In 1962 glass companies were told they had to make a better windshield. But they had a problem on their hands. If the glass broke easily, it would cut people severely on the head and face. And if it were very strong and did not break at all, the impact would cause brain and neck injuries. The new glass would have to have "bounce." Hundreds of glass pieces were broken before testers found one that worked. A plastic layer sandwiched between two layers of glass had the proper bounce. When testers dropped a weight on it, the tough plastic layer bulged out but did not break. Since 1966, all automobile windshields have been made with the new kind of glass.

Meanwhile, ordinary windows were causing trouble. Store owners kept police busy with calls to catch the smash-and-grab artists who had tossed a brick into their display windows and grabbed what valuables they could reach in a hurry. By the time the police arrived, the thief was long gone. The shopkeepers needed large windows in their stores, but they wanted a stronger glass for them.

At about the same time, many home-owners began complaining. The large glass doors they had thought to be so attractive when they had first bought their homes were turning out to be a big headache—in more ways than one. Not only were the glass doors making it easier for thieves to break in, but

(Top) *Testers use a 100-pound bag to see how easily a would-be thief can smash ordinary window glass*

(Bottom) *The same bag cracks, but does not shatter, a new kind of glass*

LIBBEY-OWENS-FORD CO.

they were causing serious injuries. A running child, weighing less than 100 pounds, could crash through a glass door easily. Housewives were afraid to keep their doors too clean, because it was dangerous for a door to look open when it was really closed. Some home-owners in the country were startled to have an occasional deer come crashing through their bay windows. What everyone needed was much stronger glass.

That meant making it thicker. Researchers began experimenting with glass from ¼ inch to 1 inch in thickness. One company broke over a quarter million dollars' worth of glass before they were satisfied their tests were complete. One test included testing the glass with a vacuum that bent the glass until it broke. When the researchers found the glass they wanted, they tried a few more tests. A 100-pound bag (to simulate a running child) was hurled against the new glass. It cracked but didn't shatter. Even when the test crew tossed three homemade bombs, it didn't break. Chopping it with a fireman's ax didn't smash it either. The scientists began to wonder just what *could* break it. They tried to smash it every way they could imagine. What finally succeeded is, of course, a secret.

The results of destructive tests are not usually called upon to be testimony in court. But it can happen. A woman had died when she fell from the 90th floor of her apartment building. But was it suicide or murder? To find out, testers set up a window like hers in their destructive laboratory.

65

Testing the new kind of glass included everything from throwing homemade bombs to trying a fireman's ax

LIBBEY-OWENS-FORD CO.

Vandalism is another crime that destructive testers try to fight. Philadelphia recently had to pay a bill of $310,-000 for broken trolley car windows in one year. Almost all the damage had been done on a trolley line that went through one bad section of the city. What could be used in place of glass windows on those particular trolley cars?

When one manufacturer discovered a heavy plastic window with a coating that would not scratch, the testers went to work on it. They had to try to think like vandals to find ways to destroy the new windows. Finally they decided that the new plastic could withstand almost any assault. As a final test, the

The window the woman fell through had been double-paned insulation glass built to withstand winds up to 100 mph. She weighed only 125 pounds. And the apartment she lived in was small. Even with the hall door open, she could have run only a short distance. She could never have gotten up enough speed before hitting the glass to break the window. The testers had to use a weight much heavier than the woman to break the window. They were sure she must have had some "help" in falling through it. But the state attorney's office decided there was room for doubt and so the case was never decided.

Will a new acrylic-type window get scratches all over? A tester checks with steel wool

E. I. DU PONT DE NEMOURS & CO.

66

This new jet took off and landed more than 36,000 times without ever leaving the ground

LOCKHEED-CALIFORNIA CO.

windows were installed in a few trolley cars that were sent through the bad neighborhood. In spite of the usual rocks thrown plus other tricks of vandals, there was only one broken window all year.

Twenty million dollars is a lot of money to spend on two airplanes that will never fly, will never take on passengers, will never be seen by more than a hundred people, and will end up on a junk pile. But the builder of these two jumbo jets figures they were a real bargain.

A few years ago many airlines were talking about buying new planes. But they could not make up their minds what to buy. Should they all invest millions of dollars in the new supersonic transports that could fly faster? Or should they buy larger jets that could carry three times as many people? One airplane manufacturer decided to build an entirely different type of jumbo jet that would be tested as no other airplane in history ever had been.

A jet that is entirely new has to prove itself. It must meet all the standards set by previous jets and also pass all the tests required by the Federal Aviation Administration. Until it passed, not one passenger could go aboard. The manufacturer built eight of his new jets. Six of them were for testing in actual flight. The other two, costing over $20 million, would be tested to destruction.

They had to answer many questions that could not be answered any other way.

"How many years will the new jets last?" asked the airline officials who might want to buy the new type of plane. "Will they still be working ten or fifteen years from now?"

No one could wait ten years to find out. The manufacturer knew he would have to give answers to those questions before anyone bought his new jets. So Jet #7 was chosen to be "fatigue-tested." It was encased in a cocoon of steel girders. Hydraulic jacks pushed against its sides to simulate the stress the same jet will feel as it taxis down the runway, takes off, climbs, has its cabin pressurized, cruises, runs into turbulence, descends toward the land-

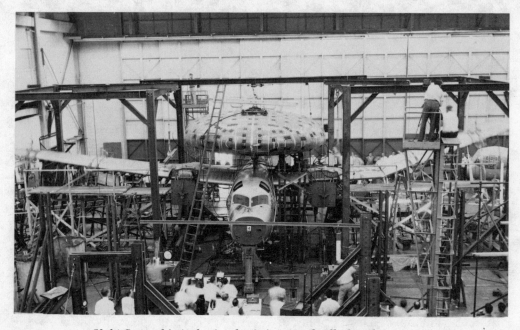

Ugh! Scrunch! And a jumbo jet's wing finally breaks

ing field, has its cabin depressurized, and makes a landing. Sometimes Jet #7 "flew" with a full load, sometimes not. Some "flights" were higher or longer than others. Every "flight" was designed to simulate the actual use the plane would have—except that there was no rest for Jet #7. No sooner had it "landed" than it was taxiing out the runway to take off again, with the hydraulic jacks simulating trips as true to life as possible. Twenty-four hours a day, every day for two years, Jet #7 flew."

While Jet #7 was getting fatigued, gauges inside monitored all the places where fatigue might show up first. If gauges showed too much strain anywhere, it was not too late to change some of the design. If any cracks were to develop, now was the time to find out. After 20,000 "flights," Jet #7 had undergone the same wear as if it had been used for 15 years. It was not worn out yet. The tests kept on because testers had to know how many hours each part of the plane would be in good working order. After 72,000 "flights," Jet #7 was still going strong.

Meanwhile, Jet #8 was not having much more fun. It was also surrounded by a network of steel girders with the same hydraulic jacks to push it around. Its job was to be tested to see how strong each individual part was. But the worst was yet to come. After the testers found out how strong each part was, they began to wonder how much more load each part could take. Twice as much? Three times? They kept loading more until each portion they were testing reached the breaking point. Someday it might be a matter of life and death for a pilot to know his plane's endurance limit, and the tests were just the way to find out.

5

Vibration, tension, and compression tests
SHAKE, STRETCH, AND SQUEEZE IT

EVERY MATERIAL made by man is subjected to different kinds of stress. Some are jiggled and shaken to see how much vibration they can take. Some are squeezed to see what compression does to them. Others are pulled, twisted, and flexed to see how much tension they will stand.

One September day in 1586, it was hard to tell where the tension was the worst—around a crowd of people or around the monument they were trying to raise. The whole fiasco had actually begun a very long time before.

The Romans were noted for helping themselves to anything they wanted when they conquered a new country. Emperor Gaius Caligula was no exception. He wanted an Egyptian obelisk. So sometime during the first century, the Roman legions had managed to transport that obelisk across the Mediterranean to Rome, where it stood for fifteen centuries.

Until this September day, it had stood, as tall as an eight-story building, in a small square. Then the pope had decided he wanted it moved to the

square in front of St. Peter's Basilica. He had offered a prize to the man who suggested the best way to move it. The winner, Dominicus Fontana, had even made a scale model to show the pope how he intended to do the moving. would erect scaffolding around the obelisk, raise it off its foundation, and then carefully lower it down to its side onto a cradle. Very gently it would be moved to its new location. All this had been done in April.

Now the day had come to raise the obelisk at its new site. Fontana had tested every stage of the job that he could think of. He had even tested the ultimate strength of each of his ropes before he decided how many men to assign to each rope. At this point, he thought, he would have given anything to know how those Roman soldiers had succeeded in raising the obelisk back in the first century. Or how the Egyptians had done it a thousand years before that! Nine hundred men and horses stood waiting for his signal.

First came religious services. Then the people were warned not to make a sound. Any noise from a bystander and he was off to prison. Fontana took a deep breath and gave the signal. The capstans began to turn. The ropes stretched and groaned. A strand of one of the ropes snapped. Then another.

Suddenly a sailor named Bresca could stand it no longer.

"Wet the ropes!" he shouted.

Amid all the tension, Fontana had forgotten something that every sailor knew. Wet ropes are stronger under tension. The sailor who had saved the obelisk was rewarded by not being sent to prison for breaking the silence. The obelisk still stands today where Pope Sixtus V wanted it.

One of the ways by which materials can be tested is vibration. But there are many different ways of vibrating. A food product manufacturer may put his cereal boxes in a carton and vibrate them for several hours to see if they can stand a long trip in a freight train without falling apart. But an automobile manufacturer has other ideas.

At least part of a new automobile's life is spent being shaken up on a vibrating machine. Loose nuts and bolts may drop on the ground beneath or, if the car is especially well made, it might not even rattle after such an experience.

One automobile manufacturer used a vibrating machine as part of his advertising. He was tired of people saying his car rattled and squeaked after a few months' use. So he had a television ad made showing a gauge that indicated how quietly his motor ran. Then he vibrated the car on a shaking ma-

A new car gets a bad shaking under the left front wheel

SCHENCK TREBEL CORP.

chine and ran it on the road again. The gauge still showed that the car did not rattle. But this was not a real test—it was only staged for the customer who wants to buy a quiet car.

When a new car gets out to the proving grounds and takes the outdoor tests, it gets more vibrations. Special roads are designed to jostle it mercilessly. One company engineer even designed a test road of cobblestones like one he had found on a trip to Belgium.

Vibration machines are doing their part to help fight pollution. As long as automobiles pour into the centers of cities every day, each one carrying only one or two people, the air will be filled with carbon monoxide and other gases produced by the auto exhausts. Many people interested in helping the envi-

71

ronment think it makes much more sense for commuters to use trains—and they are right. But one of the worst faults of trains is their vibration. Unless a passenger holds his book shaking up and down in front of his face at the same rate of speed his body is shaking up and down, he can't even read. New kinds of trains, like the new air-cushion vehicle, that ride more comfortably are being tested on train-sized vibration machines.

Vibration testing is important to set standards for builders, because nature has its own huge vibration machine! Not only do earthquakes shake buildings, there is more movement than just shaking. A building is heaved around and twisted as if the earth it stands on had suddenly become an ocean wave instead of solid ground. The Earthquake Engineering Center at the University of California has a "shaking table" the size of a small room for testing

This new high-speed air-cushion train undergoes vibration tests

what happens to buildings during earthquakes.

The only other way to test what happens to buildings when the earth trembles is to read the reports from engineers who test buildings after an earthquake occurs to see which ones survived and which ones will have to be torn down. After the disastrous quake in Managua, Nicaragua, on December 24, 1972, engineers were surprised that some of the buildings were still standing. Even engineers can be amazed when some of their inventions work just right! Some of the newest skyscrapers were almost undamaged. Yet the city all around them was flattened. A 511-block area was ruined. Thousands of people were killed in their sleep when their houses fell in on them.

One thing which had helped to keep the tallest buildings in the city from collapsing was that they had been designed especially for such catastrophes. Just forty years before, there had been an earthquake in the same city, and the builders had studied what happened that time before they put up the skyscrapers. The recent earthquake was almost a replay of the earlier one. While most of the new designs stood up well through earthquake, some of them did not. Engineers and building designers learned new lessons from nature's vibrating machine.

Sometimes tests for compression and tension are done at the same time. A bridge, for example, has both kinds of stresses.

A 1920 sandbag test for drainage pipe contrasts with today's scientific press capable of ten times as much pressure

INTERPACE CORP.

73

Anyone who has ever laid a plank over a stream of water knows how the board sags when he walks out on it to the middle. He is never sure until after he passes the center whether that "bridge" is strong enough to hold his weight. The plank sags because there are two kinds of stress on it—compression and tension. The top of the board is under compression—that is, forces squeezing or pushing together. The underside of the plank is under tension—forces stretching or pulling apart.

Every bridge must be designed with strength enough to handle the tension and the compression it will undergo. If a plank across a stream looks as though it might break when someone heavy steps on it, placing it where a stone in the water can help to support it gives the bridge a brace. This really turns it into two spans instead of one. The areas under stress are shorter, so they are stronger. That is what bridge builders do when they put piers in the rivers to support their bridges.

July 2, 1874, dawned hot and muggy in St. Louis, Missouri. But few people were thinking about the heat. It was too important a day for that. This was the day when St. Louis would begin to be as important a city as Chicago. The whole West of the continent was waiting to be settled, but the wide Mississippi River was right in the way. Ferries could move only a few people across at a time. At long last, the "Big Muddy" had been conquered by a bridge, but until this day, the bridge had never been tested.

74

The river hurries past St. Louis at a tremendous pace. The bridge builder, James B. Eads, had even descended in a diving bell to try to find a place to build the piers to hold up a bridge. He felt sure that with two piers in the middle of the river, he could build a bridge with spans a little more than 500 feet long. But he needed to build with steel to make his plan work. Other engineers and bridge designers were shocked. Steel? Why not wrought iron? It was not as strong as steel, but they had used iron successfully in bridges before. Some influential men even tried to have Eads thrown out of his job. But Eads had made tests and he insisted on a steel bridge.

Now, after more than five years of work, Eads' steel bridge was to have its first test just two days before its grand opening. For more than a month the bridge had been the most popular place to take a walk. Carriages and bicycles had used the upper bridge deck, and that traffic had tested it very well for compression and tension. But, Eads wondered, how could he test it for vibration? A moving load puts much more stress on a bridge. Then he thought of trains.

The day of the big test there were cheering townspeople lining the upper deck. On the lower deck where the railroad tracks ran, heavy locomotives began chugging toward the center of the bridge. Eads could arrange for only fourteen locomotives, so the rest of the tracks were filled with coal cars. The trains pulled back and forth across the

*Now that airports need longer runways, they also need bridges
for their jumbos to cross highways*

bridge all day. Later, Eads learned that one of the locomotive engineers had panicked and put his engine in reverse. All day long, he had been pulled across the bridge in reverse. But the test was a success.

Some bridges have traffic that the architect had not planned for—jumbo jets. An automobile driver near certain airports can look up to see a jumbo jet crossing a bridge over top of him. The sight is a little unnerving the first time, especially when the roaring motors overhang the bridge. Many tests had to be made to be certain the bridge could take the weight and vibration from a jumbo plane. Researchers found that when a jumbo starts up, it uses about 70 percent of its power to begin rolling. For this reason, the jumbos are not allowed to stop on a bridge when they are loaded with fuel—not so much because of what might happen to the

bridge but what might happen to the poor motorists driving underneath when the uproar begins.

Today bridge builders do not wait until after a bridge is built to test it. The testing is done on scale models of the bridge or on various materials used to build it. But even though testing is done carefully, there can still be mistakes.

No one wants to build another "Galloping Gertie." Gertie was better known as the Tacoma Narrows Bridge. It was a slender suspension bridge built across the narrows of Puget Sound in 1940. Because of the winds in that particular spot, Gertie had been built to be flexible. In fact, it was so flexible that the workmen building it often went home complaining of being seasick.

After the new bridge was opened, tourists drove out of their way for a ride on the galloping bridge. Four

75

months later, Gertie was heaving so badly in a 40-mile wind that it had to be closed. The last car out on the bridge held a reporter and his dog. Suddenly, as the wind caught the bottom of the bridge deck, the roadway began twisting and vibrating. The reporter tried to yank his dog from the car, but the animal was frozen with fear and would not budge. At last, the man had to abandon his dog and struggle back down the writhing bridge. He could not walk or run but had to claw his way back to safety just before Galloping Gertie's entire center span collapsed into Puget Sound.

Civil engineers wanted to learn as much as they could about Gertie's accident. They knew the wind had been the cause, but the design was at fault too. The wind was pushing against solid girders instead of open-work trusses that might have acted more like a sieve for the wind to blow through. The next time a suspension bridge was built in a windy place, it was much stronger than Gertie, though there was much less solid steel for the wind to push

A cookbook has to be tested for those many times its pages will get yanked and flipped . . .

MEREDITH CORP.

76

against. And half the roadway was built on open grids. The driver could see the water through the road—but more important, the wind could blow through the road instead of against it.

Another kind of stress that many materials must be tested for is bending. Flexion tests are designed to see what happens when things are bent or flexed.

A cook would never believe that she is so rough with one of her tools that testers had to build a special machine to check it. No book has to put up with the beating that a cookbook takes. Its cover has everything from molasses to matches dropped on it. Its pages get flicked with fingers covered with dough. And a half hour before company arrives, the book is likely to be thumbed through wildly by a frantic cook looking for a last-minute recipe.

At least one company prepares its cookbooks for the traumatic life ahead once the books leave the shelf of a bookstore. The pages are flexed 100,-000 times on a machine called a page-flex tester. They are yanked, flipped, and stretched for hours at a time to make sure they will not tear easily.

In another department, a tensile strength tester stretches a sample piece of denim material until a thread breaks in it. Measuring instruments record the strength of the force that broke the thread. This is the way testers can tell whether a popular material like denim, which is usually made into blue jeans, can be strong enough for other uses. A furniture maker wants to cover chairs with the dungaree look. An automobile

A researcher stretches a new kind of nylon stocking to measure the strain it can take
E. I. DU PONT DE NEMOURS & CO.

maker thinks he can sell some cars with the denim look. So testers try mixing nylon or polyester threads in with the cotton to see how much stronger the material can be made.

Denim is very strong material—one reason why so many workmen wear jeans. But a certain construction worker had not planned on making a test when he showed up for work on the job site one morning. Somehow a crane snagged its hook onto the pocket of his pants and whisked him out of the window of the building.

"I was dangling 52 stories above the street," he laughs now when he tells the story. The pocket held tight. As soon as the crane operator realized what had happened, he gently lowered the man to a safe spot. There are better ways to test tensile strength.

77

Another kind of stress that strains materials is twisting. Tests to see how much twisting something can stand are called torsion tests.

When a baby grabs a toy, he doesn't just pull. He twists and bends it. So when toys are tested to see if they are safe for young children, some special machines are needed. One tests a toy for torsion pull. The toy is put in the machine, and the machine gives it a twist. The gauge shows whether it was a 10-pound pull, for a young child, or more. Another is the bite machine. A metal jaw holds the toy and pulls at it with the same weight that a child of any age would be able to pull with his own teeth clamped down tight. A toy that advertises on its label "for children 12–18 months" should be able to stand the torsion and bite tests of an eighteen-month-old child.

Because of torsion and the problems it can cause, about 140,000 high school football players would have had knee injuries after the football season this year, if it were not for Dr. Bruce Cameron of Houston, Texas. He was unhappy about the many knee operations he had performed one year. The human leg is designed perfectly—even for playing football. But the designing did not take into account the sort of shoes football players would be wearing. Cleats on the bottoms of football shoes dig into the ground. That is great for traction when the player is running.

But the cleats anchor his foot firmly to the ground so that when he is hit from behind and twists suddenly his thigh bone is likely to go one direction and his shin bone the other. That is when the knee ligaments get stretched and torn.

The doctor and his associates began to study torsion to find out just how the injury happened. Next they designed a pair of football shoes with a new cleat plate that would swivel. This would allow the foot and shoe to move in the direction of the force so that the knee would not be injured. The first boy to test the new design was "Zipper Leg." He had another name but had already had so many knee operations that he was called that nickname by everyone who knew him. "Zipper Leg's" football career was ended before he was out of high school. But when he tried the new shoe, he found there was hope even for him. He played football his whole senior year.

Until Galileo showed the way, nothing that moved was ever tested. People thought of testing a bridge, but never of testing it with the traffic moving over it. They tested walls that held up buildings, but never with a force like an earthquake moving those walls. Galileo tried to show the scientists of his day that those stresses made a lot of difference in whether a material could be called strong enough to do the job it had to do.

6

Chemical analysis

TAKE IT APART

Wʜᴀᴛ could a pottery mug, an oil painting by a Spanish artist, and flakes of dried paint from an old house have in common? They were all killers and their victims suffered from lead poisoning.

Testing is not all violent and exciting. The chemist in his quiet laboratory often can do the testing when no other way will work. He actually takes things apart to find out what is in them.

When a little boy died mysteriously, his doctor thought he had detected signs of lead poisoning. He visited the boy's parents one day in the hope of discovering the killer in time to save other children.

But if the doctor had expected an easy search for the poison, he was mistaken. The parents were not poor. The child's toys had been chosen carefully to be sure none were painted with a lead-based paint. There were no signs of broken plaster or chipped paint in the house. There was not a single trace of the villain the doctor knew must be there. He asked about the child's regular habits. Every morning the boy had

drunk his grape juice from a special mug that his parents had brought home from a trip to Italy. At that point the doctor nodded sadly and left, taking the mug with him to be tested in the laboratory.

Mugs very much like that one had hurried the fall of the Roman Empire. When the rich Romans of early days had begun dying of some unknown disease, no one knew what caused it. They did notice one strange thing, though. Poor Romans never got the disease. Now we know why. Only the rich could afford to eat and drink from the lead-based pewter mugs and attractive glazed pottery plates that were fashionable then. The poor drank from goatskins and ate from unglazed clay dishes.

Some kinds of glazing compounds used on pottery contain lead. If the lead salts in such a glaze are not applied just right and fired at exactly the right temperatures, the poison can leach out into a person's food. Acidy foods are most likely to cause the lead to leach out, especially if they are warm

79

This Oriental cooking pan could be twice deadly. Testers look for lead in the lining as well as test the deadly gas that escapes when charcoal is burned in the bottom unit

U.S. FOOD AND DRUG ADMINISTRATION

and allowed to stand. This includes fruit juices, soft drinks, coffee, tomato products, cooked fruits, and foods with vinegar, such as pickles, salad dressing, and mustard.

Lead does not kill right away. That is one reason why it is such a hard killer to catch. The lead collects in the body until a certain amount has been reached before the symptoms start to show.

There is no way pottery can be tested at home to be sure that it is safe to use, but a laboratory can find out within an hour. Federal inspectors test the pottery that is imported to be sure it is safe before it can be sold in the United States. But, except for taking it to a lab for testing, there is no way people can be sure the pottery they buy in other countries or from a small ceramic shop in this country is safe, unless it

80

is labeled that the glaze contains no lead.

Lead poisoning can also come from paint made with lead. Francisco de Goya was one of Spain's most important artists when he became ill and almost died in 1792. For more than a year, he was partly paralyzed, half blind, and so mentally confused that he could not paint at all. When his strange symptoms at last disappeared and he was well again, his paintings suddenly changed from nice family portraits to grotesque figures. Art historians had often wondered why there was such a change in Goya after his illness.

No one was ever sure what Goya's sickness was, but recently a psychiatry professor tracked down all his symptoms and added to them the unusual techniques of painting that Goya used. He had always mixed his own paints, and his favorite, white lead, was most often used on his canvases. He was noted for scooping up his paint and spreading it with a rag or even his fingers. Lead can enter the body through the pores. The psychiatrist decided that lead poisoning had been Goya's problem.

Unfortunately for Goya, the doctor's diagnosis came over one hundred years too late. Thousands of city children are luckier. They can be saved from death or brain damage if their families know how to look for lead-poisoning symptoms.

Nearly all children who have lead poisoning also have another disease called "pica." The word "pica" (mean-

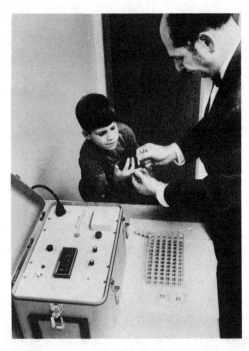

A few drops of blood to test for lead content can save a child from brain damage or death

ing "magpie") was chosen by a six-teenth-century doctor who found that some children eat like magpies—the birds that will eat anything and everything. Children with pica will eat any material that is unfit to eat. They will nibble on a piece of plaster or chew the paint off a windowsill. Houses built before 1950 are most likely to have dangerous lead-based paint in them. Since then, lead-based paint has been limited to outside painting only.

Lead is hard to find in the human body because it may be hiding in the bones and tissues as well as in the blood. But there are ways to test a child quickly and easily. One company

invented a machine that can detect lead using only one drop of blood. Although the lead may already have left the child's blood and gone to the bones or tissues, it has left behind a chemical called protoporphyrin. This chemical glows under an ultraviolet light. Best of all, the new ways of detecting lead are cheap and quick, so a city can afford to offer the test free of charge to the children of poor parents.

There is a way to test the paint from your own windowsills with a system the U.S. Navy uses: Scrape off bits of the paint into a small container. Add a few drops of sodium sulfide in 8 percent aqueous solution. This chemical can be bought in hobby shops or any store that supplies chemicals for a chemistry set. (Always keep any chemical out of reach of small children.) If the paint you are testing has lead in it, the drops of sodium sulfide will turn dark very quickly. But this test will not tell you how much lead is in the paint. Or how much your small brother or sister has eaten.

Lead is only one of the deadly things a chemist can detect. The life of a person is at stake when testing involves studying some drugs that are already inside his body.

An ambulance races up to the hospital emergency door. It is met by a team of doctors and nurses. The stretcher is lifted out as smoothly as if it were floating. A girl about fourteen lies unconscious under a blanket.

"Looks like an overdose of drugs," a policeman reports to a nurse. He had

81

found her lying in the street. He has no idea who the girl is or where she lives. But that is not important just now. What matters at this moment is what drug or drugs she may have swallowed.

The doctor shakes his head. Treatment must begin at once, but the treatment depends on knowing exactly what she has taken. If it were one type of drug, he might order oxygen. For another, she might need the kidney dialysis machine. With no treatment, she will die.

"There was no bottle lying near her? Or anything that might give a clue to what she has taken?" a nurse asks.

The policeman is sorry, but he can't help. The doctor takes a blood sample and orders it rushed to the hospital lab. There, the blood is put into a gas chromatograph. Providing that the drugs the girl has taken are of a certain kind (not arsenic), the gas chromatograph can separate the different components. Then the separated components go to a second machine, the mass spectrometer. There they can each be analyzed as perfectly as if they had fingerprints. In less than an hour, the doctor knows what the girl has taken and how much of each drug. Thanks to two new machines invented for testing, this young girl may have a second chance at living.

An agent on the trail of a drug pusher carries a quick-testing kit in his pocket. He may have only a minute or two to decide whether the man he is following is really a pusher before he makes an arrest. Just a few grains of the drug will tell the agent that he is on the right track. He adds the suspected white powder to a small plastic vial containing reagents that will change color. This test is only enough to arrest the pusher, but it is not enough to take him to court. For one thing, the vial has to be thrown away after the test because the reagents may eat through the tube. And there goes the evidence. After the man is arrested, more tests are made in the lab and the strength of the drug is determined. The stronger the drug, the higher up the scale of pushers the arrested man is. If the drug is pure heroin, the narcotics agent knows he has caught a top man. Later the chemist who did the testing in the lab must testify at the man's trial.

Most people think there is nothing much healthier than a vitamin pill. Yet recently vitamins had to be taken apart to show parents exactly what is in them.

It all began when some famous cartoon characters got into the vitamin-pushing business. Their vitamins looked like candy and sometimes the television or radio announcer even told children they tasted like candy. They meant well. Vitamins are very good for children. But as few as thirty-five of them eaten all at once could put a small child in the hospital. One four-year-old boy spent two days in a hospital's intensive care unit in a coma. He had eaten a whole bottle of iron-fortified vitamins so that he would "grow big and strong like the man said on television."

Many children and adults died be-

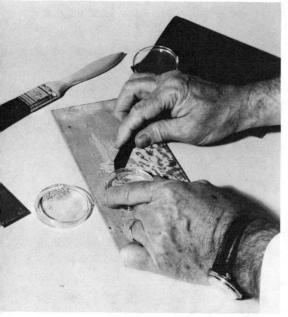
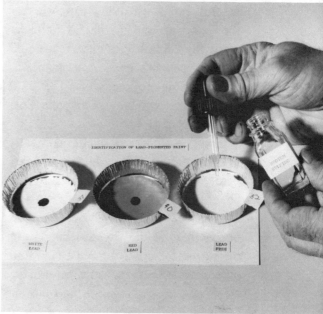

*Scrape a little paint from a windowsill, a piece of furniture,
or any painted object a child may chew on . . . A drop of
sodium sulfide on the paint will turn black or dark-gray if the
paint has lead in it*

U.S. NAVY

fore someone finally tested patent medicines—the kind people could buy already made up in a drugstore—to find out what was in them.

"Give your baby Syrup of Poppies" said one advertisement a hundred years ago. The syrup was meant to soothe and relax fussy babies. Another ad of that time told mothers to use "Infant Preservative" if their infants cried. Both "medicines" contained deadly opium!

People were dying more often from the medicines meant to cure them than from whatever ailed them. Some of the bottles contained dangerous drugs without any warnings on the labels.

Others were not much stronger than colored water, yet it was claimed on their labels that they could cure everything from hangnail to cancer! Since 1938, laws have required makers of patent medicines to tell the truth—the whole truth—on their labels.

Some old-fashioned fathers who would not allow their daughters to use makeup may not have been completely wrong. The cosmetics used by the ancient Egyptians, Romans, and Greeks were made by doctors. But a few hundred years ago, doctors got too busy to make eye shadow and lip rouge, so the job was done by anyone who wanted to try. Some companies were careful, but some didn't care whether they used arsenic in the face powder or in the eyelash darkener that could infect a person's eyes. A woman was taking a big chance when she used makeup until the Food, Drug and Cosmetics Act of 1938.

Today a modern cosmetics company tests its products for one to five years before the customer ever has the chance to buy them. Testing begins as soon as a new formula has been decided on. If there is the slightest change in the formula, the testing must begin all over again. Every product must have a self-sterilizing safeguard built into it. For example, a moisturizing cream is sterile the day it leaves the factory. But if it is used by a person with dirty hands or if the lid is left off so bacteria can multiply, the cream is no longer sterile. A self-sterilizing agent in the cream helps keep bacteria from growing even under the worst of conditions.

All the time a new product is being tested, it sits on the company's shelf under a code name. "Ajuj," "Tuesday," "Lunik," and "Snoopy" will never appear in advertisements. The chemist who invented those cosmetics may give them their code names, but when it comes time for them to go out into the world, new names will be selected to match their personalities.

After the new cosmetic is finished, it moves to another shelf—this time in the microbiology laboratory. For three to five months it will sit there waiting for the test to show whether bacteria have grown in it. If they have, it's back

to the first lab for more tests until the bacteria count stays down. Tests in the "weather room" will show whether tropical heat or an Arctic blizzard cause any chemical change in the product. What happens to the cosmetic in high altitudes, what effect exposure to the sun has on it, and what might happen after it spends years on a bathroom shelf are also tested by chemists.

People with allergies are happy about a law passed in 1973 that requires cosmetic companies to state on their labels what chemicals are in their products. Until now, those people had to buy only nonallergenic cosmetics. Today, if they know which chemicals they must not use, they can read the labels and treat themselves to some new products they would never have dared try before.

Since long before the first Earth Day, many chemists in laboratories have been testing pollution. But for many years, there was not enough information or the right equipment available for taking apart air and water to see what was in them.

About thirty years ago, a chemist living on the St. Clair River, near Detroit, had his own system for measuring water pollution. He took his boat, the *Juicy Scoopy,* out in the river and collected some water for a pot of tea. If the tea didn't taste right, he knew that the water was polluted. But he had no way of knowing exactly *what* was in the water or how much of any one pollutant was dangerous to people. Worst of all, there was no one to complain to.

84

Today, when a complaint reaches the Environmental Protection Agency, the staff have many ways to find out what is in the pollution. They can even find out which factory let the pollutants into the air or water. They take apart the samples chemically, using some new helpers like the gas chromatograph and mass spectrometer.

You can make your own tests by collecting water samples from a stream near a company you suspect is polluting. Be sure to collect a sample of the water both upstream from where the factory releases its effluent, or material, out of its sewer and into the stream as well as downstream. Label the samples carefully. Next collect a sample of the effluent itself as it drains from the pipe or overflows from the company's holding basin.

The actual tests should be made in a chemistry lab, so you will need your science teacher to help. If you find serious pollution, notify your nearest EPA office. Your tests can help convince them, but the tests cannot be used in court against a company. In order to prove a case, the EPA investigators must seal their own samples in the presence of witnesses before they leave the scene. Then the samples are kept locked up in the lab, so there can be no question later about whether the sample was tampered with.

One of the products that chemists are trying to test has been around since the beginning of time. No one knows yet just what is in smoke to make it so deadly.

When a fireman bursts into a burning building, his greatest danger does not come from the flames. The smoke and the gases hidden in that smoke concern him the most. Eight out of ten firemen's injuries are from *gas* inhalation, not from smoke inhalation as many newspapers report.

No fire has one single gas that is dangerous. There are always several. That is what makes it hard for a chemist to analyze smoke and fumes. Even in a controlled test, some of the very dangerous gases might escape notice. Some gases are dangerous only in combination with another. Some are dangerous only when a certain temperature is reached. Gases are produced either with or without smoke. Some gases make the eyes water, so a person escaping cannot see where he is going. Different gases come from the different materials that are burning. Many plastics give off especially poisonous fumes. A burning warehouse, filled with a wide variety of materials, may even give off such deadly gases that people must be moved from houses half a mile from the fire.

Although there is no test yet that can tell all the gases that are in a burning room, researchers can test the gases that they know are present at every fire. Carbon monoxide is one of these. Until recently, no one knew a great deal about the gas known to chemists as CO.

Carbon monoxide has a unique way of killing people. It makes a person breathe much faster, so that he takes in all the poisonous gases present at a faster rate. The red blood cells in the body will absorb carbon monoxide 210 times faster than they will take in oxygen. Chemists found that even a little bit of CO in a person causes him to lose his sense of time and to make faulty decisions.

A lot of chemicals have been turning up in the wrong places. This is not a brand-new problem. The well-dressed gentleman of about a hundred years ago wore a beaver hat—if he could afford one. Medical books in those days warned people they might have headaches from the hats, or even might lose their hair. The men who made beaver hats were already suffering from strange symptoms. The Mad Hatter from Alice in Wonderland's tea party was modeled from what people knew of hatters in those days. Unfortunately for the hatters, it was many years before someone discovered they had mercury poisoning from chemicals used to treat the beaver skins. About the same time, chemists discovered that the pretty colored-sugar candies that boys took along when they went calling on a girl were actually poisonous. The colors came from such goodies as lead, copper, mercury, and arsenic. Even a child's paint box in those days had arsenic and copper in the colors.

Today mercury is still popping up in the wrong places. Twenty years ago, a strange thing happened in a Japanese fishing village. All the cats of Minamata began to walk crooked and act peculiar. A few years later, many peo-

ple began having trouble when they walked too. Then some lost their eyesight. Others had brain damage and became cripples. At first, no one knew whether something was wrong with the air or whether they all had some odd disease or whether the trouble was caused by something they had all eaten.

Tests were made on everything—until the researchers came to the fish that were the daily diet of both the cats and the people in the village. They took the fish apart and found an unusually large amount of mercury inside. The contaminated fish had fifty parts per million of mercury. The standard for safety set in most countries is one part per million. In the United States the standard is only 0.5 part per million.

The Japanese researchers learned that a local plastics factory had been dumping its waste, full of alkyl mercury, into the same bay where the people of Minamata had fished all their lives. In those days people thought it was safe to dump anything into a large lake or bay. No one ever tested the lake afterward. The waste had disappeared and therefore it must be gone, they thought. Now we know that mercury does not lie harmlessly at the bottom of the water. It gets into the fish food chain and comes right back inside people.

Just a few years ago mercury appeared in swordfish. Then in tuna fish. Then in fish caught in Lake Ontario. Soon people all over the country were worried about eating fish. The Food and Drug Administration is a govern-

An FDA inspector makes sure that rellenos (a Puerto Rican favorite food) are made under sanitary conditions

ment group whose duty it is to see that the food eaten in this country is safe. When tests showed there was mercury in some fish, the FDA took the contaminated fish out of the markets. Even today no one is quite sure how much mercury people can eat and still be safe. But someone had to set a limit somewhere, so the FDA limit in the United States is set lower than in other countries.

Bacteria that get into food are another target of FDA inspections. The inspectors do not wait to be invited to visit a food-canning or freezing plant. They just show up suddenly one day and begin checking out what happens to food before it reaches the grocery store. What they learn is sometimes shocking.

One day they may watch vegetables being put into containers to be frozen. Several containers are set out on trays, so they can be carried easily into the quick-freezing room. The containers are sterile. The food is clean. But what about those trays? They are often stacked on the floor until they are needed. Then in the freezing room the trays are stacked one on top of another like a pyramid. The dirt from the *bottoms* of the trays drops into the clean food. And freezing will not kill bacteria.

Bacteria tolerate cold, but they thrive in warm temperatures and the moist environment around warm food, multiplying rapidly. That is why frozen-food packages often say "Do not defrost before using." The less time they have to warm up, the better.

One company that freezes packages of chop suey learned that the hard way. They had made the chop suey one afternoon and stored it overnight in shallow pans in a refrigerator room. The bacteria count then was 600 organisms per gram—not too bad. By midmorning, as the chop suey was warming up, the count increased to 1,500. But work was slow that day, and by early afternoon many trays of chop suey were still sitting around at room temperature. A bacteriologist took two more samples to count. One had 320,000 organisms per gram. The other had 660,000! Now the workers hurried and packed the rest of the chop suey in small packages

87

and raced to the freezer with them. But instead of being frozen quickly as in a small home freezer, the packages were all stacked into large cartons. Then the cartons were put into the freezer for blast-freezing. It takes much longer to freeze a carton. By the time the packages of chop suey were ready to leave for the grocery store, the bacteria count tested from 5 million to 10 million per gram! Fortunately, that chop suey never got to the store.

Another thing the FDA tests find in food which should not be there is dirt. Not all foods are prepared as carefully as people cook in their own kitchens. One family bought a loaf of bread and discovered that it had been neatly sliced up with a whole mouse (also neatly sliced) inside it. When they reported the bread to FDA inspectors, the bakery was closed quickly. There were mice and rats all over everything at that bakery.

An old proverb says that everyone eats a peck of dirt during a lifetime. The human body can take care of a little bit of dirt, evidently. But recently the FDA published their list telling how much dirt they think is too dirty. They call a one-pound jar of peanut butter "contaminated" if it has more than 225 insect fragments (pieces of insects) or 10 rodent hairs in it.

Another job of the FDA labs is to see that food labels tell the truth. Chocolate ice cream cannot be labeled "chocolate" unless it has no artificial flavoring in it. If most of the flavoring is artificial, the label must state "artificially flavored chocolate." But the federal laws control only ice cream made in one state and sold in another state. If sold only in the state where it is made, the product can be called chocolate ice cream and show a tiny sign somewhere on the label that states "artificial flavors used."

You can try making your own ice-cream test the way the Consumers Union testers do. Remember: you are not supposed to be eating the ice cream for enjoyment this time. You will be taking it apart.

Vanilla ice cream should have some tiny black specks—they are bits of the vanilla bean. Cut into the ice cream with a spoon. It should not be gummy, sticky, or crumbly. Press down with a spoon. The ice cream should not be like snow or dough. Put a spoonful in your

If rats have been near these bags of pinto beans, the FDA inspector's "black light" will detect traces of rodent urine

mouth and press the ice cream against the roof of your mouth. There should not be any ice crystals or icy spots on your tongue. Hold a bite in your mouth and let it slowly melt. After the cold wears off, there should be a sweet aftertaste. Don't get carried away—this is not a taste test! Let the rest of the ice cream melt in the dish for fifteen minutes at room temperature. Then look at it. It should still be creamy and look the way it did when it was frozen. If it looks like frothy soup or has turned to curds and thin liquid, it certainly isn't the real thing. Try buying another brand next time.

7

Nondestructive testing

HANDLE WITH CARE

IN THE OLD DAYS the only way to find out what was inside a product without destroying it or taking it apart was simply to look at it. Unfortunately this method was only as good as the eyes of the person who did the looking.

Nondestructive testing is designed to discover flaws that could cause trouble —before they have a chance to cause accidents. Luckily, the nondestructive tester does not have to depend on his eyes alone. There are many new instruments that can do a much better job.

One helper is the X-ray. Radiography can make things reveal their innermost secrets. In almost five centuries no human eye had ever noticed that a famous painting by Titian, hanging in the National Gallery of Art in Washington, D.C., was actually three paintings. The picture shows Venus and Cupid in front of a mirror. But Venus is hiding something. Underneath her painted figure is a portait of a man and woman. And underneath them is still another painting—the first scene that the painter had put on the canvas. Titian is not the only painter who could

90

not make up his mind. In a portrait of an old woman by Giuseppe Ribera the X-ray showed that there was once a little girl in the lower left-hand corner. The old woman's hand was once above

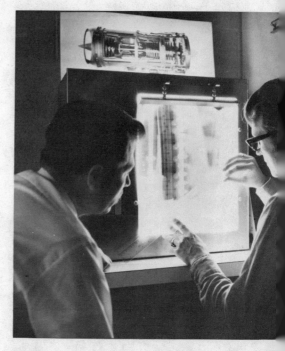

Radiography helped an airline discover an engine problem that could have cost thousands of dollars

E. I. DU PONT DE NEMOURS & CO.

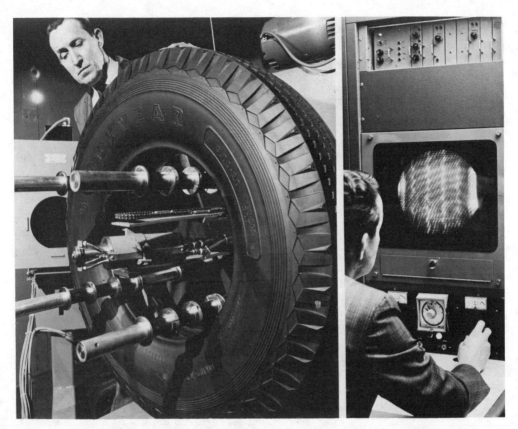

X-ray shows the tester what he cannot see inside a steel-belted truck tire

GOODYEAR TIRE & RUBBER CO.

the child's head as if she were saying, "Here is my little girl." But the art gallery visitor cannot see any hint that a little girl is beneath the dark paint under the woman's hand.

The X-ray helped an engineering professor with a riddle that had bothered him for many years. He had an Egyptian ax almost four thousand years old. He had always called it a ceremonial ax, but his friends insisted that it was a building tool. He could have proved they were wrong by trying to chop wood with it, but he would have

ruined his ancient artifact. Instead, he had it X-rayed. The radiograph showed that gas in the casting had allowed the ax to become porous inside—it could never have been meant to chop wood.

Radiographs can be made with other rays besides X-rays. A radioisotope produces a ray that penetrates even heavy steel. Recently a small airline sent its airplanes for a routine inspection that included using a radioisotope. A hidden flaw was discovered that could have caused engine damage in time. The airline officials were grateful that the testing had included radiography. Their airline has never had a single accident!

Radiography helps airport inspectors trap hijackers, too. Inspectors know what is in a woman's purse or a student's backpack before they even open it. A new invention helps them to locate even plastic explosives that are hidden deep inside a suitcase. Bags may travel on a conveyor belt past an X-ray machine. A television camera picks up the picture on the fluorescent screen and sends it into the inspector's office via a television screen. With that kind of system, the suspect's suitcase may be far away from the scene of action, but the inspector can be standing right behind the prospective hijacker within seconds.

Holography is one of the newest helpers for the nondestructive tester. When the idea for a 3-D photograph was born over twenty years ago, its inventors had good reason to feel discouraged. Holograms would work, but

Testing the world's fastest car has to be nondestructive

only with a special kind of light. And the right light did not come along until the laser beam was invented. Now specialists in many fields keep finding exciting new uses for the hologram.

An oceanographer may wonder how plankton or tiny fish travel through the sea. When an underwater camera was dropped into the center of a plankton colony, some of the sea creatures were always out of focus and all of them were disturbed to have a camera in their midst. But a hologram taken of a colony is different. Each tiny organism can be seen in perfect detail. Each individual in the colony is as clear as if the whole group had been suddenly frozen in its travel.

Nondestructive testers use holograms to find out what happens to droplets of oil inside an engine, or to see what the inside of a tire looks like. A hologram of a tire shows up defects as clearly as knotholes show in a pine plank.

Racing cars are carefully tested at every stage while they are being built. But once they are on the track—at the Indianapolis 500 or at Daytona—they are carefully checked over by a nondestructive tester in the pits. He has a small portable unit to quick-check the axle and steering gear before a race. *The Blue Flame*'s racetrack is on the salt flats of Utah. Last-minute testing was a must before it took off to set a new world's land speed record. Its driver, Gary Gabelich, reached 622.-407 mph.

People who think automobile test drivers always lead exciting lives should trade places with one nondestructive tester. His job is to see that a new car model passes the government test for nonpollution. In this case, it's not what the car can do, but what comes out of its exhaust pipe that matters. The pollution cannot be seen by the eye accurately enough to suit the government standards, so a computer takes over the job.

The driver buckles his seat belt and pulls the shoulder harness across his chest, not because he is going to drive fast but because he is going so slowly he may get hit from behind. Most of the time kids on bicycles will zip past him. When he speeds up, it will be the kind of slow crawl that drivers should use traveling through a school zone. Then he will hit the brakes, stop, and creep up to a tortoise crawl again. This goes on for days—until the car has chalked up as much mileage as if he had driven from Maine to Southern California.

Back at the test lab, the car rests twelve hours in a garage where the temperature and humidity are carefully controlled. Next day the car engine is turned on and its exhaust is trapped in a large plastic bag. A computer records how many parts per million of hydrocarbons, carbon monoxide, carbon dioxide, sulfides, nitrogen oxides, and other components are in that exhaust. If the car fails the test, it goes back to the drawing board, because a new law says that cars can no longer pollute the air.

If the car passes the test, its fate is

almost as bad, because it is back to the road again for another slow-motion 4,000 miles. This whole process is repeated until the new motor has traveled 50,000 miles and can still pass the computer's exhaust-pollution test.

Another good tool of the nondestructive tester is the subsonic wind tunnel. Although most people think of this testing ground being used with aerospace experiments, it has many other talents. One of them is testing golf balls.

Golf can be traced back to the days of the Romans. They used a bent stick to hit a leather ball stuffed with feathers. By 1457, a Scottish king found that his people had been spending so much time playing "golfe and futeball" that they had been neglecting their archery. Since he was counting on their prowess with bows and arrows to keep enemies from invading Scotland, he had no choice but to declare both games illegal. But soon after, gunpowder became popular for wars, and archery was no longer of much use. Golf came back to stay.

The golf balls used then were called "featheries." They had been made by wrapping leather tightly around wet goose feathers. But after the feathers had dried out, the balls often burst when hit and showered the course with feathers. A Scottish minister invented "gutties." They were made of gutta-percha, a gum from a Malaysian tree. They did hold together, but they also had a disadvantage. They flew far out when hit and then suddenly plummeted straight down to the ground. Golfers soon found that after the "gutties" had been nicked a few times, they traveled farther than new ones. Soon golf ball makers began putting the little nicks on when they made them. Such balls did travel farther—so much farther that golf courses had to be made larger. But there had to be a limit. The space on the earth for golf courses is not endless. So the ball was limited in size and weight. Now the only things that could be changed were the materials used to make the balls—and, of course, the dimples on it.

One company asked an aerospace professor how it could make its ball fly farther than any other. He tested many

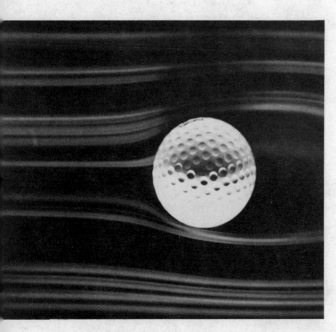

Wisps of smoke help researchers see the lift and drag of a golf ball in a subsonic wind tunnel

94

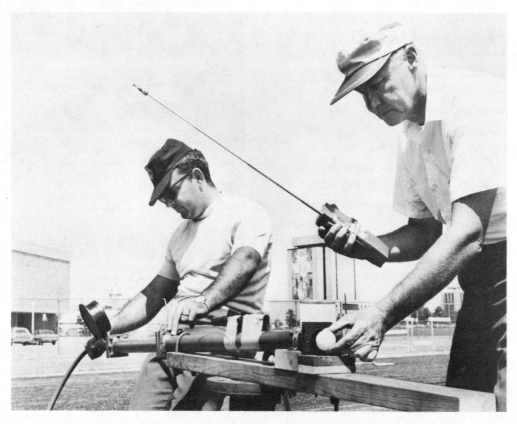

A gadget that "drives" golf balls, a high-speed camera waiting for the action, a radio to contact the cameraman, and a computer—all help to test a golf ball

UNIROYAL, INC.

old balls in a subsonic wind tunnel so he could make comparisons. Some had round dimples, some had diamond shapes, squares, or cones. It was impossible to tell with the eye which balls had the best lift and the least drag. But by using over-sized balls in the wind tunnel, the professor could see there was a lot of difference in action between balls—mostly caused by the shape of the dimples.

The professor took some newly de-signed golf balls out onto a golf course. He built a machine that, unlike a person, would hit each golf ball exactly the same way. After many hours of testing and using a computer, the ball with the hexagonal-shaped dimples beat all the others.

Occasionally nondestructive testers let their eyes help them spot flaws. One way to find a defect in a metal piece is by using the magnetic particle test. First the metal is subjected to a strong magnetic field. Then it is covered with tiny particles of metal. These arrange themselves carefully around every part that is magnetized. But where there is a crack there will also be a break in the magnetic field. The tiny particles of metal avoid the crack area, so the flaw can be seen by a trained inspector.

Ultrasonics can be used also. High-frequency impulses—too high to be heard by the human ear—are sent through the metal and picked up on a scope. Modern architects often use steel plates over 1½ inches thick in building skyscrapers. Such large pieces of steel may hide the same weakness as the Egyptian ax—impurities such as trapped gas. Or tiny cracks may start inside the steel after it has been welded. Later the cracks may become much larger. In case of an earthquake, a small crack could become very serious. Fortunately, cracks in completed buildings can be repaired after ultrasonic inspection has located them.

Many times nondestructive testers have used a high-speed camera to spot what their eyes can't see. "Moving pictures" actually got their start because there were so many badly crippled soldiers after the Civil War. Their only hope, after losing a leg on the battle-field, was for a clumsy wooden leg and a cane. But one doctor knew he should be able to do better than that. First, though, he had to know exactly how people walk.

Since high-speed cameras had not yet been invented, he set up sixteen cameras—each one set to go off a split

96

A glass "road" and tire treads painted white will help testers find out how tires squirm at high speeds. Note movie camera pointed upward toward the tire

GOODYEAR TIRE & RUBBER CO.

second later than the camera before. When a person walked normally in front of the battery of cameras, the doctor had what amounted to a "moving picture" of the way a person walks. He could then design an artificial leg that could copy all the body motions of a person walking.

Today, high-speed movies can take up to 44,000 pictures in less time than it takes to snap the button once on an Instamatic. A manufacturing company was having trouble with a machine used to sort cards. The selector kept picking up one card when it should pick up two. When the engineers slowed down the machine, it worked perfectly. Only when it ran fast did the selector keep making mistakes. For nine weeks engineers tried to find out what the machine was doing wrong. By the end of that time, they had decided that the selector was bumping the card pile out of line. It was out only about 2/1000ths of an inch, but that was enough to throw the entire machine off. The cards were moved ever so slightly—but had the movement been to the left? to the right? or up? or down? or in or out? The eye could not tell.

Finally the company brought in a high-speed movie camera with a macro-lens that made the small cards look like stacks of lumber. With the movie camera taking pictures at 11,000 frames per second, the engineers could see exactly what was happening. After that, repairs took only a few minutes.

Another high-speed camera shook up a group of engineers recently when they decided they had better have a closer look at a dam they were building in Virginia. Many test borings had been made in the hillsides that formed the two abutments on either side of the new dam. But the hill on one side appeared to have some caves in it. Several of the engineers had argued that it was only one long cavern and they had just kept putting the bore holes down in the same cave. Others were afraid there might be many caves that could fill with water and cause the dam to break some day.

To solve the argument, a very special kind of camera was hired. It would fit down a 4-inch-wide hole and carry a telescopic zoom lens. Because the engineers knew exactly how long it would take the zoom lens to focus on a rock underground, they could estimate just how large the cavern was. A powerful miniature floodlight provided light for the cave pictures. The camera sent up its pictures to a closed-circuit television. What it showed surprised even the engineers who had expected to find holes there. The inside of the abutment looked more like Swiss cheese than a mountain!

The camera was lowered into many different holes until the engineers were certain they had taken the measurements of every single cave. After they had filled each cave and changed the shape of the dam slightly, the project could be completed safely. They were glad they had not depended on either their own eyes or on the bore holes to spot flaws.

These are just a few of the new discoveries which help the tester without hurting the product he is testing. Any one of them would have been far beyond Galileo's dreams. He would have been happy just to have had an accurate clock when he began testing materials.

Since he could not rely on his clock to count exactly sixty seconds to a minute, Galileo used something that he could rely on—his own pulse, which beat seventy-two times per minute. He set a pendulum, a weight suspended on a thread, that also beat seventy-two times per minute. Another of his timing devices consisted of a bronze ball that

What's at the movies? In this case, about 80 days of ultrahigh-speed movies of automobile safety tests

rolled down a wooden track. He could set it for "fast time" or "slow time" simply by changing the slope of the track. To measure the time it took the ball to go down the track, he used a water clock. Water dripped through a small pipe into a glass as the ball descended the track. When it landed at the bottom, Galileo stopped the clock and weighed the water that had collected. Simple arithmetic compared the different "water times."

8

Testing with people

TRY IT OUT

A TESTER cannot really say he has "tried everything" until he has tried testing his product the way it is going to be used. The ultimate test is to try out an item in a real situation with people.

"Trying it" used to be the only test there was. A bridge was proven safe after traffic had crossed it without its collapsing. The first iron ship passed the final test when it was launched and did not sink after everyone said it would.

The final test of George Westinghouse's air brake was not planned to be a matter of life and death. The only way to stop a train before 1869 was by teamwork. The engineer, seeing the tracks washed out ahead or a train parked on the same track, began tooting his horn wildly. The brakemen, hearing the signal, leaped into action. Each raced toward the nearest hand brake and began tightening it as fast as he could. Each car had its own brake. In the few seconds before a crash, the brakemen had to step lively to tighten as many brakes as possible.

"There has to be a better way," Westinghouse muttered to himself one day when his train was delayed at the scene of a crash.

His invention actually began in a fun house at an exposition. Compressed air, rising through a hole in the floor, lifted women's skirts—sometimes as high as the ankle—and blew men's hats off. Westinghouse decided to use that same compressed air to stop a train's wheels.

For the real test, Westinghouse had borrowed a four-car train to prove that his brakes would work. Railroad officials who had been invited to watch the test were ready to be impressed—they knew how badly train brakes were needed. The test train, with everyone on board, chugged out of a tunnel in Pittsburgh, Pennsylvania, on the way to the testing place. Suddenly the engineer saw a horse-drawn wagon standing dead still across the tracks ahead. He tooted the horn. The horses panicked, reared, and bolted ahead so abruptly that the driver fell over backward. He landed motionless across the tracks.

The engineer twisted the brake valve frantically. The train ground to a stop —just four feet on the safe side of the unconscious man. The new brakes had passed the surprise test.

As soon as people are added to testing, the unexpected happens, because people really are unpredictable. The same products that did exactly what they were supposed to do when tested for impact, vibration, tension, or other strains, may behave quite differently when people are added to the testing. The president of a power mower company found this to be true when his advertising manager suggested lending some of their power mowers to people in the community.

"Then we can ask the people how they liked our mower and use their

Companies must test power mowers by doing all the wrong things that people may do when they take the mower home
THE TORO CO.

100

words in our advertisements," he added.

"Or if they have complaints, we can make improvements," another company official said.

The idea sounded great and soon the hum of several mowers was heard on lawns outside the factory fence. But when the investigator from the company called on the people using the lawn mowers, he found that people do the unexpected. One man was using his lawn mower to chew up sticks. Another had cut his leg badly because he ran the mower over a concrete curb and was hit by a piece of the broken blade. And at still another house two men held the mower up in the air, trying to trim the hedge with it.

Testing the customer as well as the product is not a bad idea, because a company loses money when a dissatisfied customer returns the product. Companies lose even more money when someone is injured using their products. The law courts often decide in favor of the person who was hurt— even though he may have been using the product the wrong way.

"We even have to tell people not to vacuum puddles of water," said a vacuum cleaner maker. "Before, we used to just wonder who in their right minds would do such a thing. We can make our machines safe, but we can't idiot-proof them."

New York City's trash department spent two years in testing to find a wastebasket for the city streets. The old wire mesh ones were being stolen at the rate of six thousand a year—although no one could imagine who would want one. They never had held the litter very well. Besides, people kept dumping garbage in them.

One hundred new containers were tested on the streets. The choices had been narrowed down to four styles—twenty-five of each. After seeing what people did to those, the trash department narrowed the choice to one model. But this one still needed to be tested with people. First the trash department made the mistake of putting it up too high. Trash collected underneath it. Since it weighed almost 500 pounds, the container was not easy to clean under. Then the hole in the top was too big—people stuffed their garbage in as before. The problem of cost was the easiest one to solve. Containers were made hexagonal in shape, giving each one six sides that could be used as advertising space. So the new containers pay for themselves.

Archaeologist Hans-Ole Hansen had some unique products he wanted to test with people. As he looked over the ruins of a village two thousand years old, a few rusty tools, and some broken bits of pottery, he suddenly had an idea. This had once been a living village. Why couldn't it be again? If he could put people back in it, even if they were twentieth-century people, couldn't he learn much more about life two thousand years ago?

In 1964, Hansen began his unusual research center at the village of Lejre (pronounced: lie-ray) in Denmark. Instead of turning the site into a museum

of artifacts, he would make a village come alive as no one had ever done before. Only a living person could prove whether a flint scraper found in the village would actually scrape a small animal skin. Only living people could prove that the clay ovens found near one house foundation were meant to smoke meat by actually trying it. There were small pieces of wool clothing found near some skeletons that had been discovered on the site. But the wool was of a strange type. Only a living person trying to weave the same sort of textile could prove that the wool had been made by people of this village.

Hansen found eighty young students —from all over the world—who were just as excited about the project as he was. They began rebuilding six of the houses, carefully following the ground plans that were already there. They used the same Iron Age tools the original people had used when the village was first built. Archaeologists showed the modern builders the old post marks where a double row of posts through the center of the houses had held up the roofs. But what shape should the roofs be? Since they had been thatched, there was no evidence at all left for the young builders to guess about them. So each house was finished with a slightly different slope to the roof. One of the six should be right.

At last the most important part of the test started. The students tried living in the village. Three of them actually moved into the rebuilt houses, but they found that the twentieth-century builders did not know quite a few things that the Iron Age builders had known. How to keep the roof from leaking, for one thing. How to make the smoke go out through a smoke hole, for another. But Hansen was not discouraged. His students were proving exactly what he had wanted to prove—that archaeologists who simply drew pictures of ancient homes from the skimpy evidence they found in the ground could never be sure they were right. Only real people living there could find out.

Meanwhile, students at work on other projects in the village were having more success. Hansen had some of them building a loom for weaving that was exactly like other looms found at ancient sites. They already had the pieces of wool textile for a sample. But no one had ever put the two together. Could that kind of loom make that kind of wool material? First, they had to find out where the wool had come from. There were bones of a very small kind of sheep found in the ground near there. But could such a small sheep produce that kind of wool? To find the same kind of sheep, they had to import animals from the Faroe Islands. A girl used their wool and made a cape so much like the original bit of material found in the grave that Hansen knew he was on the right track.

Another team made pottery, using only the materials that could have been found nearby in the Iron Age. Their pots were so much like the originals

that they had to be marked to tell them apart. Another team planted all kinds of primitive grains and found that the ancient plows were much better to use than anyone thought they would be. Hansen's testing with people proved much about historians' theories—that a lot of them are right and just as many are wrong.

One kind of testing that cannot be done at all without people is tests that use the senses. No computer or other machine can really tell a researcher whether something tastes or smells good.

Taste-testing is not so simple a matter as sitting down to enjoy a new recipe. It has to be done scientifically. There are too many pitfalls for the unscientific taster. He is sure, for example, that a dark-chocolate cake has a stronger taste than a lighter one. To prevent mistakes, the taster's laboratory has dull lighting. Most people taste the first bite of a food more than any bite after it. So the lab has plenty of ice water and saltines on the table for tasters to eat in between tests.

Some testers find that the facial expressions a person makes when taking a bite can affect the people around him. Tasters usually sit facing the wall. They are not supposed to make grunts of "Yeccch!" or squeals of delight. Some labs even separate their tasters by dividing the counter into small cubicles so they cannot see each other's faces or plates.

You can try the "triangle taste test" to see which of your friends has the

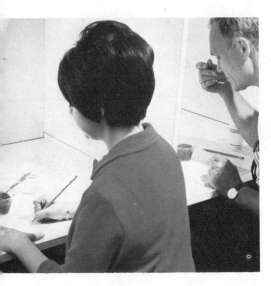

*Tasters trying the same food are separated
so they cannot influence each other*
GOOD HOUSEKEEPING INSTITUTE

If you're not good with cakes, try a test with three kinds of dessert topping —the frozen kind, the dry powder you mix yourself, and the old-fashioned whipped cream. Or try the same flavor of four kinds of drinks—a grape soda, grape punch, grape juice, and powdered grape drink. Or a contest between boy cooks and girl cooks—to see which are best in your school. If you try this one, be prepared for a surprise.

When a food company decides to try out a brand-new product, it collects a small group of people together. A group of teen-agers may be asked what they think is the messiest job in cooking. Melting the chocolate before they can make fudge? A lot of people said yes to that one, so researchers were sent off to think up ways of selling premelted chocolate. When a way is found, it is tried out in homes. If the new product passes the family test, it is ready to move on. Now, instead of making up two hundred packages of the product, the company will make enough to sell in one "test" city. A test city must be large enough to have its own radio, newspaper, and television station to carry the advertisements. If the new product is popular with people in the test city, it may be tried across the nation—just for a limited time. There are good reasons for being so careful about introducing a new product. Freeze-dried coffee was tested for two years because, if it became a success—which it did—the company would have to build entire new factories in order to make it.

most educated taste buds. Bake two chocolate cakes, using different mixes or recipes. Give each friend three samples of cake. Don't tell anyone that two of his three pieces are from the same cake. Make sure the tasters face different directions so they can't read each other's faces.

Now have the tasters fill out a questionnaire on their three samples. Which did they like best? Which had the best texture? Which was moister? How do they compare the first sample to the second and third? At the very last, ask which two pieces of cake were the same? To save time, you can use the Smiley Scale that some of the professionals use instead of writing answers: a round circle for a face, two button eyes, and a mouth with a turned-up or turned-down smile.

103

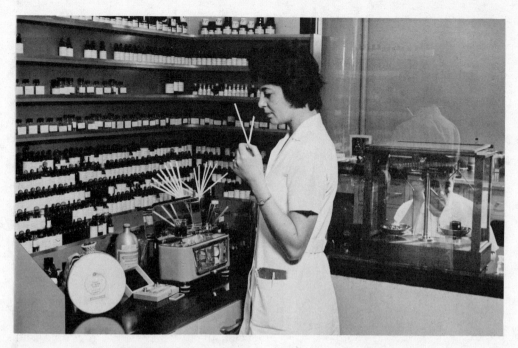

No machine works as well as the human nose for smell testing

Jasmine . . . sandalwood . . . nutmeg . . . ylang ylang . . . tuberose. Even without knowing what all those words mean, a person can guess that they smell good. A company that makes perfumes has dozens of scents to choose from. But no machine can tell what smells good to people. Instead, the company must use real noses.

Fragrance-testing rooms have isolation booths where the nose can smell only one thing—the perfume being tested. Everything affects a perfume's odor—even the temperature of the room. The same scent smells different on different people. To make matters worse for a perfume company, once they find a popular fragrance, people want talcum powder and bath soap that

104

smell just the same. But the element that makes the perfume smell is not so easily transferred into powder and soap. The testing depends on educated noses, even though a computer can tell the makers what ingredients to put in the product.

Smell testers are not sure where they stand right now in the war on pollution. One Iowa city says that no technological gadget in the world replaces the human nose. They employ seven "unbiased citizens with a good sense of smell" to check out complaints of bad odors in their town. But the engineers in Philadelphia say there is no point in hiring certified smellers because there are just too many bad smells around!

The sense of hearing makes people

useful to scientists testing for noise pollution. America has become a very noisy country. Machines measure noise in decibels, but doctors are learning that noise pollution cannot be measured in decibels alone. Just living where it is noisy can cause enough stress to make people sick. They cannot sleep because decibels that would hardly be noticed during the daytime can disturb them at night. Hikers at the top of Mt. Rainier—14,410 feet high —can hear the diesel trucks at night on a highway forty miles away.

Other countries have noisemakers, too. Norway banned snowmobiles because they were too noisy. In Tokyo, Japan, where most of the construction work is done at night, there are noise-measuring devices on some of the main street corners. Zurich, Switzerland, shuts down noisy factories for two hours at lunch time and twelve hours during the night. There, even lawn mowers must have mufflers and trash cans must be made of quiet materials. But Moscow is one of the noisiest cities in the world. The racket on the subway platform is 100 decibels. That is worse than a jet airplane landing.

You can try a test which the U.S. Department of Housing and Urban Development sometimes uses to check whether a building site is going to be

"Saturday morning noise" test for a lawn mower

THE TORO CO.

too close to traffic noise for comfortable living. First, find a friend whose hearing and voice are about like yours. Then take along a 100-foot tape to measure distance and something to read aloud—not a book you both know by heart, but something unfamiliar. Choose a time when the traffic is at its worst. Or test the same place several times during the day.

Have one person (the speaker) stand on one spot with something in his hand to read. He should read in just a normal voice, not shout. The other person, holding the tape measure, faces the speaker and slowly backs away. At some point, the listener can no longer understand every word. When he reaches the point where he can understand only a few scattered words during a ten-second period, he measures the distance between the speaker and himself.

To be accurate, the listener should make several tries and mark the distance each time, taking the average distance. Also, he should trade places with the speaker to see whether his measurements are the same.

If the listener was standing less than 7 feet away when he could no longer catch more than a few words, that site is hopeless. If he was between 7 and 25 feet, it would cost too much money to build a house there that could shut out competing noise. If the distance is between 26 and 70 feet, it will probably be comfortable inside the house. But if the listener was more than 70 feet away, both the inside and the out-

106

Forty years ago, fingernail polish came in one color—pink. The man who experimented with more colors made millions of dollars

side could be pleasantly quiet.

Color-testing is something else that depends on people and their senses. The deadest color in the world is "cotton-classing gray." It is also one of the most expensive to buy by the gallon. But there is a good reason.

Since white often picks up colors around it, the only way to test white is to put it where there are no colors— no blue sky, green grass, pink walls, not even a blue-tinted light bulb. Many old plantations had such a "cotton-classing" room where the cotton was taken to be separated. The cotton that had become stained or darkened by bad weather could be used only for dark cotton materials. The purest white brought the highest prices.

At the Good Housekeeping Institute, testers may use the color room—painted in cotton-classing gray—to see whether one white material is whiter than another. Or to see whether one kind of washing machine washed the shirts whiter. Under an ultraviolet light in the room, stains show up that are invisible under ordinary lights.

All sorts of people may be needed when it is time to have a try-it-out test. Recently testers needed a group of children under five years of age. The Food and Drug Administration had become so worried about the number of small children killed every year in their own homes by poison that they lined up their best researchers to find out what to do about it. The decision was to design a medicine bottle that children could not open. This took a lot of testing. The little people being tested were veteran bottle openers. Besides, they were all born mimics. Those who could not open a test bottle the first time were able to do it as soon as they saw someone else opening one. The new FDA rules make medicine bottles so hard to open that 85 percent of children under five cannot manage them. And even after they have been shown how to open them, 80 percent will still be unable to. At the same time, the bottles had to be easy enough for 90 percent of adults to get them open.

Another try-it-out test involved almost 800 people. An entirely new type of jet airplane with a wide body that could hold 350 passengers had to pass many tests before the first passenger could be allowed on board. One of these tests is the Federal Aviation Administration's rule that the plane must be able to be entirely emptied of passengers within a minute and a half. The evacuation test had to be done in the dark, with debris thrown in the aisles for passengers to climb over just as there might be during an emergency

Planning how to evacuate a jumbo jet and actually doing it with real people are two different things

LOCKHEED-CALIFORNIA CO.

107

landing. Although the plane has eight doors, only four could be used for the test. And the "passengers" for the test were not to know in advance which doors would open.

The test was not only to find out whether the plane could be evacuated quickly without anyone getting hurt but also to check whether the directions to the passengers were clear. Evidently they were not—because the first 355 people flunked the test. Three of the open doors were hardly used, while most of the passengers piled up at the fourth exit. That could have meant disaster in a real emergency. For the second test, 355 new people sat down in the "plane" waiting for the "crash landing." This time the directions were clear. In eighty-one seconds, everyone was out safely.

New methods of transportation have been tested in every way imaginable before being tried out with people. But getting people and things from here to there still has to be tested in a realistic way.

Just how tough was the horseless carriage? People were wondering that one bitter-cold day in 1908. A crowd had collected on Lincoln's birthday in Times Square, New York City, to watch the start of one of the world's craziest races. Six cars—three French, one Italian, one German, and one American—were at the starting line. The American machine was the *Thomas Flyer* and one of its crew was George Schuster. Schuster had been the chief road tester and he knew every

bolt and rattle in the *Flyer*. He had taken it up to 60 mph and knew that it could even climb some hills without it being necessary to change gear. The 4-cylinder engine had the power of 60 horses.

But the race was to be from New York to Paris—the long way across the North American continent, Siberia and Europe, with a boat ride in the middle. More than 13,000 miles when 50 miles was considered a long ride! Even George Schuster thought the idea was wild, but he had been offered $50 a week to go along and he was not about to pass up that kind of money.

In 1908 there were no interstate highways or expressways. Snowplows had not yet been invented. There were no gas stations or road maps. There were not even roads across most of the country. Motors had to be cranked to get started, and because cars were so hard to start in cold weather, most owners just jacked them up until spring every year. But Schuster and the rest of the American team wanted to give the race a try, even though the president of *Thomas Flyer* said they would never make it to Chicago. They packed cans of gasoline, tire patches, a 45-star American flag, goggles, shovels, picks, axes, and lanterns and searchlights to help find the roads.

A few large cities had paved roads out into the country to be used by bicycle enthusiasts. The racers were happy when they found those. In between roads, they used canal towpaths, old covered-wagon trails, muddy farm-

108

A test car enters the straightaway that is level for 3½ miles

GENERAL MOTORS CORP.

ers' roads, and even railroad tracks. Once the crew, scheduled as a "special train," had one too many flat tires as they bumped over the railroad ties and had to set out flares to stop the onrushing express train. There was a canvas to protect the men from heavy rains— because cars had no roofs then. At one place, the *Thomas Flyer* driver had to invent a seat belt to keep himself from being thrown out as they jogged over rocky trails.

One night in July the *Thomas Flyer* crew discovered they were ahead of the few cars that had survived the race. They were entering Paris at the head of a victory parade when a policeman stopped them. They had no headlights. The crew tried to explain—of course, they had no headlights after 13,000 miles. But the policeman insisted that they must have headlights or else! The other cars were just behind. The finish line was just ahead. Schuster found a French cyclist in the crowd with a light on his bike. He hustled the Frenchman and his bike into the front seat, switched on the light, and proceeded.

San Francisco is noted for steep hills. At the proving ground is a copy of one of its worst streets

Today when people ask how tough an automobile is, testers usually take it to an automobile proving ground. There are special roads there for certain kinds of testing. A gravel road gives the driver a chance to try out the shock absorbers on a car. A 3½-mile straightaway that is absolutely level—within a fraction of an inch—lets the driver test fuel consumption and wheel balance. Even the smallest rough spot is smoothed away by hand on a 4½-mile circular track. The cracks between the paved sections are not allowed to cause a bump. The same sort of care

110

is given to the worst section of the track. There the caretakers cultivate 4 miles of the worst cement and asphalt, the nastiest potholes and tooth-rattlingest bumps to be found anywhere. A test street duplicates a street in San Francisco that makes a ski jump look tame. One proving ground has 80 miles of roads to test how its cars will behave after they leave the factory.

The proving ground gives a car a trying-it-out test, but to find out how a car behaves with people required another test. The Consumers Union has a different way of testing a car. First, they buy the test car from a dealer without telling him what they plan to do with it. After buying one car of each make, they test the cars against each other. This way they can tell people which car gets the best gasoline mileage or which car would be best for a farmer who needs a pick-up truck or which car suits a family with a lot of children. Often the testing engineers find problems the car's maker never noticed. One car had window washers and a container for the washing liquid, but no connection had been made between the two. Another made a terrible noise. When the researcher took it back to the salesman, he called it "a quirk in the new engine." The quirk chewed up two complete sets of gears. Testing cars with people can be very educational— for the testers as well as for the manufacturers.

If any place in the world needs a new method of moving people and cargo, it is the frozen north. The trucks and bulldozers that serve man so well in other climates behave like monsters in the Arctic. They leave marks on the tundra that can never be repaired. When oil was discovered on the North Slope of Alaska, men hoped to ship out the oil by sea. But ships cannot come near the harbors because the water, when it is not frozen solid, is too shallow. A machine was needed that could take the place of a car, a truck, and a boat.

The air-cushion vehicle is all of those. But it had begun life as a pleasure boat to carry sightseers over rivers and lakes. Many tests had to be made to see whether it could stand Arctic life. The ACV (its shortened name) hovers over a surface on a cushion of air. It rides over snow, ice, muck, swamps, or water. Its makers tried making it larger and found that it can carry twenty-five tons. When it moves over the delicate Arctic tundra with a heavy load, it doesn't leave as much of a mark as would a single footprint. Besides, it can be taken apart, loaded on an airplane, and reassembled somewhere else.

Small ACV's—just large enough for two people—could take the place of automobiles in the Arctic. But these are also finding a place in other climates. Air cycles (small ACV's) are being tested now as the perfect machine for every sport on snow, marsh, water, or dry land. But first the air cycle needs

The air-cushion vehicle is tested on the land . . .
and on the water

BELL AEROSPACE CO.

111

Checking the way the ACV can be taken apart, shipped or flown to another area, and put together again

to be tested with people, because it is very different from wheeled vehicles or boats.

One of the very newest forms of transportation is thousands of years old. But no one is about to buy one at a local boat show. The test of this new boat, built of papyrus, was not supposed to start a new trend in shipbuilding. This test was for history.

Thor Heyerdahl had often wondered about the similarities between the ancient people of Egypt and those of Central America. Aztec legends told of a god who had come from another world to become their leader, and Heyerdahl felt that he knew where that god had come from because of the secrets he

112

had brought to the Aztecs. Yet, Egypt and Aztec country were separated by a cruel and dangerous ocean. If there had been an exchange of knowledge, it had to come *from* Egypt, and a boat had to be the missing link.

What bothered most historians was that neither country had any boats— unless one could call the Egyptian papyrus raft a boat!

"No papyrus boat could possibly sail across the ocean," they had argued with Heyerdahl.

But the anthropologist had located boats made of papyrus in both the Old World (Africa) and in the New (on a lake between Peru and Bolivia). In fact, finding the papyrus boat in South

America was another of the mysteries that supported his point. But he had to admit that in both places, the natives had said their boats would not last more than a few weeks in water. They had to take them out of the water to dry out when they were not in use. And the ocean trip, Heyerdahl reasoned, would have taken many weeks.

But he could not give up his theory. Not if he had to build a papyrus boat and sail it himself across the ocean to prove that it could be done. It would be a dangerous test, but the danger did not worry Heyerdahl as much as did the design of the boat. A boat went in only one direction in those ancient days—with the wind pushing. So it could only

have sailed from the Old World to the New—because that was the direction the wind blew. In the tombs of Egypt he found pictures and models of the boat he had in mind. The *Ra* was named for the Egyptian sun-god.

Even at the very moment the boat was ready to sail, there were objections.

"I tried soaking papyrus in my own bathtub," said a friend who was president of the Egyptian Papyrus Institute. "It sank in a matter of hours. Please don't go."

But Heyerdahl was not to be turned back. He and his crew had packed the boat much as an ancient Egyptian sailor might have. There were jars for water and crates of chickens for fresh

Thor Heyerdahl built the Ra I *and the* Ra II *to test a theory*
TIMES-CHRONICLE, JENKINTOWN, PA.

113

meat. Only the radio looked out of place in the papyrus boat.

Actually, the first *Ra* came close— but did not quite make the trip. It sank and its sailors knew why. The builders, men from the African village where papyrus boats were used, had made a change from the ancient drawings. They could not see any reason to make the stern of the boat the same height as the bow, but within a few days on the sea the reason was plain enough to see. The stern began sinking.

The *Ra II* was built by men from Lake Titicaca, the only place in the New World where papyrus boats were used. This time the "paper" ship made the trip. By testing, men living in the twentieth century had proven a fact of history that could never have been proven any other way: the voyage *could have been* made.

BIBLIOGRAPHY

Here are some of the reference books and other books that helped provide background information:

Abbott, Arthur V., *Testing Machines, Their History, Construction and Use.* D. Van Nostrand, Publishers, 1884.

Britannica Book of the Year, 1971. Encyclopaedia Britannica, Inc., 1972.

Britannica Yearbook of Science and the Future, 1970. Encyclopaedia Britannica, Inc., 1971.

Clymer, Floyd, *Those Wonderful Old Automobiles.* McGraw-Hill Book Co., Inc., 1953.

Coit, Margaret L., *et al., The Growing Years* (Vol. 3 of *The Life History of the U.S.*). Time-Life Books, 1963.

Consumer Bulletin Annual. Publication of Consumers Research, Inc., Washington, N.J., 1972.

Crane, Verner W., *Benjamin Franklin and a Rising People.* Little, Brown & Company, 1954.

De Camp, L. Sprague, *The Ancient Engineers.* Doubleday & Company, Inc., 1963.

Encyclopedia Science Supplement, 1970–1971. Grolier, Inc.

Engel, Leonard, and the eds. of *Life, The Sea.* Life Nature Library, Time Inc., 1961.

Frey, Albert Wesley, *Advertising,* 3d ed. The Ronald Press Company, 1961.

Gilbert, Eugene, *Advertising and Marketing to Young People.* Printers' Ink Books, 1957.

Heyerdahl, Thor, *The Ra Expeditions.* Doubleday & Company, Inc., 1971.

Horizon, Winter 1968, and Spring 1970. American Heritage Publishing Co., Inc.

Jacobs, David, and Neville, Anthony E., *Bridges, Canals & Tunnels: The Engineering Conquest of America.* Published in assn. with the Smithsonian Institution, The Smithsonian Library. American Heritage Publishing Co., Inc., 1968.

Kirby, Richard Shelton, *et al., Engineering in History.* McGraw-Hill Book Co., Inc., 1956.

McGraw-Hill Yearbook of Science and Technology. McGraw-Hill Book Co., Inc., 1972.

Miller, John Anderson, *Master Builders of 60 Centuries.* Reprint. Books for Libraries, Inc., 1972.

Newman, James R. (ed.), *The Harper Encyclopedia of Science.* Harper & Row, Publishers, Inc., 1963.

Parson, William Barclay, *Robert Fulton and the Submarine.* Columbia University Press, 1922.

Piccard, Jacques, *Sun Beneath the Sea.* Charles Scribner's Sons, 1971.

Schuster, George, with Thomas Mahoney, *The Longest Auto Race.* The John Day Company, Inc., 1966.

Singer, Charles, *A Short History of Scientific Ideas to 1900.* Oxford University Press, 1959.

Singer, Charles; Holmyard, E. J.; and Hall, A. R. (eds.), *A History of Technology,* 5 vols. Oxford University Press, 1958.

Slonim, Morris James, *Sampling in a Nutshell.* Simon & Schuster, Inc., 1960.

Straub, Hans, *A History of Civil Engineering: An Outline from Ancient to Modern Times.* M.I.T. Press, 1964.

Van Nostrand's Scientific Encyclopedia, 4th ed. D. Van Nostrand Company, Inc., 1968.

Wilson, Mitchell, *American Science and Invention.* Simon & Schuster, Inc., 1954.

In addition to books, these magazines, newspapers, journals, and pamphlets supplied information:

An Assessment of Noise Concern in Other Nations, Vol. 1, Dec. 31, 1971. U.S. Environmental Protection Agency, Washington, D.C.

Business Week, magazine.

Connecticut Medicine, Aug., 1971. Connecticut State medical journal.

Consumer, the Food and Drug Administration magazine.

Consumer Bulletin, magazine.

Consumers Reports, magazine.

DuPont, magazine.

Engineering News-Record, magazine.

Environmental Control and Safety Management, magazine.

FDA Papers, journal of the Food and Drug Administration.

Fire Journal, National Fire Protection Association magazine.

FTC News, journal of Federal Trade Commission.

Good Housekeeping, magazine.

Machine Design, magazine.

Nation, magazine.

National Safety News, magazine.

The New York Times, newspaper.

Paperboard Packaging, magazine.

Popular Science, magazine.

Reader's Digest, magazine.

Research: Engineering Methods and Materials, Jan., 1960. U.S. Bureau of Reclamation, Denver, Colo.

Routine Surveillance for Radionuclides in Air and Water, pamphlet. WHO, Geneva, 1968.
Science, magazine.
Science Digest, magazine.
Science News, magazine.
Scientific American, magazine.
Time, magazine.
U.S. News & World Report, magazine.

INDEX

Italicized numbers indicate illustrations.